One World—Many Paths to Peace

One World—Many Paths to Peace

Inter-faith symposium with His Holiness the Dalai Lama.
Hosted by the ANU College of Law.

Published in Celebration of the 20th Anniversary of the award
of the Nobel Prize to His Holiness the Dalai Lama.

edited by Venerable Alex Bruce

eView

Published by ANU eView
The Australian National University
Canberra ACT 0200, Australia
Email: enquiries.eview@anu.edu.au
This title is also available online at: http://eview.anu.edu.au/

National Library of Australia
Cataloguing-in-Publication entry

Author: Bruce, Alex, 1968-

Title: One world-many paths to peace [electronic resource] :
             inter-faith symposium with His Holiness the Dalai Lama / Alex Bruce.

ISBN: 9780980728415 (pdf)
             9780980728408 (pbk.)

Subjects: Religious tolerance--Congresses.
             Religions--Relations--Congresses.
             Globalization--Religious aspects--Congresses.
             Social conflict--Religious aspects--Congresses.

Other Authors/Contributors:
             Australian National University. Faculty of Law.
             One World-Many Paths to Peace (2007: Canberra, A.C.T.)

Dewey Number: 201.5

All rights reserved. No part of this publication may be reproduced, stored in a retrieval system or transmitted in any form or by any means, electronic, mechanical, photocopying or otherwise, without the prior permission of the publisher.

Cover design and layout by ANU E Press

This edition © 2009 ANU eView

Table of Contents

Introduction 7
    Venerable Alex Bruce

1. Welcome 13
    Professor Michael Coper, Dean, ANU College of Law

2. Opening address 15
    Venerable Alex Bruce, Buddhist Monk, Senior Lecturer,
    ANU College of Law

3. The Buddhist tradition 19
    Address by His Holiness the Dalai Lama

4. The Catholic tradition. 25
    Address by Most Reverend Christopher Prowse,
    Catholic Auxiliary Bishop of Melbourne

5. The Jewish tradition 29
    Address by Rabbi Jonathan Keren-Black

6. The Islamic tradition 35
    Address by Professor Abdullah Saeed

7. Are religions to blame?. 39
    Venerable Alex Bruce

8. Introduction to Christianity 63
    Professor Raymond Canning, Australian Catholic University

9. Introduction to Buddhism 85
    Professor John Powers, The Australian National University

10. Introduction to Judaism 103
    Rabbi Paul Jacobsen

11. Introduction to Islam 121
    Professor Abdullah Saeed, University of Melbourne

12. The position of Tibet in international law 139
    Venerable Alex Bruce, The Australian National University

Appendix: Summary of the Memorandum on Genuine Autonomy
    for the Tibetan People 161

Participants' details 167

Introduction
VENERABLE ALEX BRUCE

In June 2007, The Australian National University's College of Law hosted an extraordinary symposium in Canberra of religious leaders to discuss the issue of religion and world peace. The inspiration for this symposium was Cardinal Francis Arinze's impassioned defence of the world's religious traditions in his inspiring text *Religions for Peace*.

In a world torn by violence and intolerance in the name of religion, the visit to Australia of His Holiness the Dalai Lama represented an ideal opportunity to bring together representatives of the Buddhist, Christian, Islamic and Jewish traditions to further the fundamental message that the world's religions are really causes for peace and harmony.

In the presence of His Holiness the Dalai Lama, representatives of the Christian, Jewish and Islamic spiritual traditions explained why their respective traditions embodied the highest ideals of wisdom and compassion and thus were not the principal cause of war and dissention within society.

For more than two hours, His Holiness the Dalai Lama, Bishop Christopher Prowse, Professor Abdullah Saeed and Rabbi Jonathan Keren-Black shared their views on the lived experience of peace and wisdom within each of their spiritual traditions. Designed and moderated by Venerable Alex Bruce, himself a Buddhist monk and senior lecturer in law at The Australian National University, the symposium, titled One World—Many Paths to Peace, provided a message of hope, reassuring the almost 6000-strong audience that there was no reason why the world's great spiritual traditions should be a source of violence and conflict.

To the contrary, each speaker carefully returned to the basic tenets of his spiritual tradition and explained how those tenets embodied the highest aspirations of humanity.

In previous addresses, the Dalai Lama has identified fundamental differences between Buddhism and other religions but has also identified the numerous similarities between many of the religious traditions, particularly in their teachings of non-violence, tolerance and spiritual development.

The speakers demonstrated that despite the differences between religions there were ways forward—through respect, compassion, friendship and tolerance—

to achieve peace in our diverse and conflicted world. The dialogue therefore emphasised the fundamental message of peace, compassion and wisdom at the heart of the world's great religious traditions.

His Holiness the Dalai Lama warned, however, against what he called 'mischievous people' in all religions—people who did not have much interest in religion, but sought to manipulate religion in order to gain political or economic power.

All of the speakers recognise that the real trouble occurs when religion is allied to nationalism, ethnic hatred and economic imperialism or simply exploited for baser motives. These counterfeit forms of religion drive deep wedges between people, tribes and nations. They prevent us from forming enduring friendships.

On this theme, Bishop Christopher Prowse notes that 'friendship is surely the ultimate answer to the misuse of religion as a false pretext for war and terror. If the perception is that religion only causes world problems and creates enemies, then friendship between us is an urgent priority.'

Nevertheless, it has to be admitted that in times past, religion itself has been employed as a means of destruction and oppression. In his address, Professor Abdullah Saeed noted that while one's religion could be likened to a garden with beautiful flowers, splendid colours and wonderful trees, the garden also had some ugly aspects hidden beneath the beauty: dead trees, weeds, thorns and the like.

In addressing those 'ugly bits', Professor Saeed noted that religious practitioners had become increasingly aware of the fundamental interconnectedness of humanity. We cannot hurt others without hurting ourselves.

This is why all religions emphasise the value of peace making. In his address, Rabbi Jonathan Keren-Black quoted rabbinical writing confirming that, '[i]n God's eyes, the person stands high who makes peace between people— between husband and wife, between parents and children, between management and labour and between neighbour and neighbour'.

In the text *Global Responsibility*, noted Christian theologian Professor Hans Kung remarked: 'there can be no peace among the nations without peace among the religions. There can be no peace among the religions without dialogue between religions. There can be no dialogue between the religions without research into their theological foundations.'

All of the speakers at the symposium reinforced the need for continuing dialogue between the world's spiritual traditions in order to understand each other and to grow in friendship and love. His Holiness the Dalai Lama outlined his 'four-point strategy for inter-religious harmony':

1. meeting scholars from different traditions and discussing similarities and differences in approach
2. meeting people from different traditions who are not necessarily scholars but to exchange their deeper spiritual experiences
3. going on pilgrimage to different holy places
4. leaders of different traditions coming together to speak the same message of love, compassion and peace.

The approach of His Holiness is very similar to the approach of the Catholic Church. In its 1991 document *Dialogue and Proclamation*, the Pontifical Council for Interreligious Dialogue outlined similar strategies:

- dialogue of life, in which people strive to live in an open and neighbourly spirit
- dialogue of action, in which Christians and others collaborate for the integral development and liberation of people
- dialogue of theological exchange, in which specialists deepen understanding
- dialogue of religious experience, in which people grounded in their own traditions share their spiritual riches.

All of the speakers at the symposium reinforced the urgency of open, respectful and honest dialogue between the world's religious traditions and saw their participation at the symposium as contributing to that task.

Another crucial aspect of this dialogue involves practitioners of all traditions sharing with each other at a fundamental level. To do this requires that we understand each other's tradition. The idea is to communicate with each other and not just talk to each other.

As part of that process, this volume includes chapters that explain the basic tenets of Christianity, Buddhism, Islam and Judaism. Experts in their fields have written these chapters for the sole purpose of presenting their spiritual tradition in as transparent and accessible a form as possible. For example, it should be possible for a Buddhist, knowing nothing about Islam, to read the chapter written by Professor Abdullah Saeed and come away with an appreciation of the basic tenets of Islam. Likewise, a Muslim, knowing little or nothing about Christianity, can read Professor Raymond Canning's excellent chapter and come away with an appreciation of the basics of Christianity.

For some people, however, the very idea of religion playing a positive role in twenty-first-century society is difficult to accept. What role can religion and religious metaphysics play in liberal democratic societies? To address these questions, I have written a chapter titled 'Are religions to blame?' The chapter traces the emergence of 'atheist humanism' that flowered from the thought of Francis Bacon, René Descartes, David Hume and John Locke. I explore the dehumanising and tyrannous results of those societies that have determinedly pushed out religion. I suggest that in contemporary Western liberal democratic societies, we are living under another form of tyranny called 'consumerist capitalism' that also has dehumanising consequences. While I do not suggest we should roll back the benefits of the Enlightenment or the scientific revolution, we marginalise religion and religious metaphysics at our peril.

One society that has openly attempted to eliminate religion is China. While China encourages 'state-sanctioned' religious organisations such as the 'Patriotic Church', it openly persecutes those it considers subversive. The situation in China is important, not just because of the vastness of its economy but because it is an emerging power in the world.

Wherever he goes, His Holiness the Dalai Lama speaks about the troubled relationship between China and Tibet. And whichever country the Dalai Lama visits, China strenuously objects to government representatives meeting with him. China maintains that the 'Dalai clique' is attempting to foment 'splittist' agendas—that is, to quietly orchestrate independence for Tibet, thus splitting the great Chinese 'Motherland' of which Tibet has always been a part.

The 2008 Olympic Games, hosted by China, ignited worldwide protests drawing attention to the continued gross human rights abuses perpetrated by China in Tibet. Many Chinese citizens were genuinely confused about why Western societies reacted so strongly.

Because it is such an important issue, I have included in this volume a chapter that considers the position of Tibet in international law. I have not simply repeated the position of the office of His Holiness, but have researched the work of many international scholars who have considered the 'Tibet issue' since the Chinese military occupation in 1950. While the chapter is a little technical, I hope that it provides material enabling further study and discussion.

Also included in the appendix to this volume is His Holiness' November 2008 'Memorandum on Genuine Autonomy for the Tibetan People' which sets out the foundations for His Holiness's 'middle-way' peace plan for Tibet and for which His Holiness received the Nobel Peace Prize in 1989.

The volume concludes with information about the wonderful speakers who made the symposium such a great success.

I invite you to read, savour and enjoy the uplifting, challenging, surprising but always hopeful contributions to this volume. May you all find happiness and its causes, may you all be free from suffering and its causes and may you all journey to enlightenment with a smile.

This volume is dedicated to the health and long life of His Holiness the Dalai Lama. May His Holiness's efforts bring lasting peace to the world and may he continually manifest wisdom and compassion in ways that are most beneficial for innumerable sentient beings.

1. Welcome
PROFESSOR MICHAEL COPER, DEAN, ANU COLLEGE OF LAW

Ladies and gentlemen, it is an honour and a pleasure for me to welcome you, on this typically wintry Canberra day, to this unique and very special inter-faith dialogue with His Holiness the Dalai Lama.

I am Michael Coper. I am the Dean of The Australian National University's College of Law, and it is a great pleasure for me to be, as it were, the 'bookends' for this event, as I shall also be closing it in 90 minutes' time.

May I first of all acknowledge our presence on Ngunnawal land. This acknowledgment is not an empty ritual. It is one way in which we can not only pay our respects to the traditional owners of this land, but also further the cause of reconciliation, by taking seriously the wonderful and ongoing cultural and spiritual contribution to this country made by Indigenous Australians generally, and, to this region, by the Ngunnawal people in particular. I invite you to reflect on reconciliation as we listen to our speakers this afternoon.

You may be wondering what the connection is between inter-faith religious dialogue and the ANU College of Law, which is hosting this event. You will be especially puzzled if your image of a lawyer is that of a technician who, for a healthy fee, merely services the legal needs of others, and is unconcerned with justice, values or morality. At the ANU College of Law, we do our best to combat this stereotype. Lawyers do need technical competence and that technical competence is the underpinning of stability in our personal affairs and our public governance arrangements.

But being a lawyer is about much more than this. At the ANU College of Law, we have an ethos of educating our young lawyers to use their legal knowledge and their legal skills to become leaders in our society; to defend the fundamental principles and values of our legal system such as the rule of law, the dignity of the individual and respect for human rights; and to work for the betterment of the law and the operation of the legal system. I think you will see at once how our mission, although secular, resonates with the objectives of inter-faith religious dialogue: we are all looking for common ground in our common task of making the world a better place.

There could be no better rebuttal of the stereotypes about lawyers, and no better testament to the broader ideals that lawyers may espouse, than the embodiment of those ideals in the persona of our moderator this afternoon. Typifying also the rich diversity that resides in the ANU College of Law, our moderator is my friend and colleague, the Venerable Alex Bruce, senior lecturer in competition law and restrictive trade practices, one-time litigator with the ACCC [Australian Competition and Consumer Commission] and Buddhist monk ordained into the Tibetan tradition of His Holiness the Dalai Lama.

Today's symposium is entirely Alex's brainchild, and the first step in Alex's longer-term plan to establish enduring arrangements for the continuation of inter-faith dialogue, so it is entirely fitting that he should moderate today's discussion. I would add only the footnote that some of you may have been expecting to see as moderator former High Court Chief Justice Sir Gerard Brennan, as that had been flagged in some of our early publicity. Sir Gerard is unfortunately unable to be here, and sends his apologies and best wishes.

It remains for me to mention only two housekeeping matters: first, to remind you to switch off your mobile phones, and, secondly, to ask you to refrain from using flash photography, both for obvious reasons, and particularly out of respect for the amenity and comfort of the participants and your fellow members of the audience.

Finally, then, may I repeat my welcome to you all, and ask to warmly welcome to the podium our moderator for this afternoon's discussion, the Venerable Alex Bruce.

2. Opening address
VENERABLE ALEX BRUCE, BUDDHIST MONK, SENIOR LECTURER, ANU COLLEGE OF LAW

Your Holiness, Bishop Prowse, Rabbi Keren-Black, Professor Saeed, Professor Coper, Distinguished Sangha, ladies and gentlemen.

Growing up in Brisbane, there were two occasions each year that I could guarantee to annoy my family: birthdays and Christmas. Each year my long-suffering family would ask: 'Alex, what would you like for your birthday, Christmas, etc?' And I would reply, 'World peace and spiritual enlightenment.'

I was a weird kid. As I grew older, my brother would give me a bottle of gin, inviting me to seek enlightenment in my favourite spirit. My sister once gave me a rock from the garden, announcing in a deadpan voice that it was, after all, a 'piece of the world'. Hmmm.

My very kind parents gave me books—lots and lots of books, which I devoured.

Over the years two quotes stuck with me. Firstly, His Holiness the Dalai Lama observed that 'we cannot create outer peace without first creating inner peace'. The second was from Christian theologian Hans Kung, who stated: 'There can be no peace amongst the world's nations unless there is peace amongst the world's religions.'

The sentiments expressed in these quotes are of course related.

It wasn't supposed to be this way in the West. The project of both the Enlightenment and the Renaissance was to create a new human order in which freedom, truth and happiness prevailed, without any transcendent or metaphysical support. Human rationality and their will to power were to be the Archimedean point around which everything in the future was to pivot.

Its success was supposedly heralded by Friedrich Nietzsche's 'madman' from *The Gay Science*, who ran through the streets screaming, 'God is dead.' But God didn't die and we might imagine God sitting with Mark Twain assuring us that 'reports of my death are greatly exaggerated'.

Nevertheless, it is fashionable these days to attack religion and its metaphysics, to loudly assert that religion is the cause of all evil, war and dissention. Religion is said to be the real enemy of democracy, tolerance, pluralism and the exercise of conscience.

The shrill rhetoric of the Christopher Hitchens of this world claims that belief in God and adherence to religion demeans us, retarding our abilities to think for ourselves and to achieve genuine happiness. For such people, the sooner we jettison the metaphysics of religion and stick to scientific reason, the better we all will be.

However, this sort of rhetoric is a lot like candy—attractively presented and sweet tasting to our postmodern sensibilities. But when scrutinised, just like candy, their rhetoric is found to be just as brittle and equally devoid of any intellectual nutrition.

Critics of religion do their utmost to widen and strengthen the separation of reason and religion. Starting from Martin Heidegger's comment that religion and reason are separated by a large gulf, critics set up reason as the ultimate source of inquiry over and against religion, which is tolerated, so long as it is practised in private, kept to oneself and hidden.

In fact the world's great spiritual traditions insist that although religion and reason are distinct sources of knowledge, each enriches and supports the other. As one leader put it, 'religion and reason are the two wings on which the human spirit rises to know the truth about itself'.

Religion without reason degenerates into subjective emotionalism and superstition. Reason without metaphysics degenerates into nihilism and self-destruction. On this point, it is highly significant that the totalitarian regimes of the twentieth century that did their utmost to destroy religion also became the most self-destructive and self-cannibalising.

The oceans of blood and mountains of corpses produced by the twentieth century were not caused by religion, but by its absence. After surveying the militantly atheistic regimes of Hitler, Lenin, Stalin and Mao, the great theologian Henri de Lubac wrote [that] it is not true that people cannot organise the world without religion. What is true is that without religion, people can ultimately organise it against themselves.

Reason alone, divorced from the metaphysics of religion, is not enough for us. Reason will provide a scientific explanation for disasters, destruction and the apparent randomness of death. And we need that. But as Karen Armstrong points out, we are 'meaning-seeking creatures' and without metaphysical narratives, we fall very easily into despair, into a nihilistic absence of meaning.

What substitutes for meaning today is the nihilism of postmodernism or the grim calculus of utilitarianism or the hedonistic pursuit of individual autonomy in vain attempts to find a lasting basis for happiness and the answers to the big existential questions of life.

In a society where anything goes in the pursuit of selfish personal autonomy, there is no sense of objective wisdom or compassion. And where people create their own values with no horizons of goodness for guidance, we witness both self-destructive choices and trivialised modes of life.

Without the metaphysical anchors provided by religion, the autonomous self and mistaken ideas of the 'I' become self-referential. In this way, the urges and dictates of the self define both reason and morality.

That which is reasonable is that which serves to satisfy my own desires. That which is moral is that behaviour consistent with self-gratification and best able to achieve my individual desires and will to power.

In this analysis, other people become means to my own subjectively determined ends. And the people whose ends are met are those with the most power. Without any recognition of or appeal to transcendent truths, the person, tribe or ethnic collective that has the most power gets to determine what is meaningful and reasonable. Those who don't fit—the weak, the vulnerable, the ethnically differentiated or those who go to the wrong church—are quickly marginalised, or worse.

War, totalitarianism and genocide are simply expressions of a stronger party's conclusion that it is both reasonable and necessary to eliminate those who do not satisfy the tenets of the 'New Reich' or 'Cultural Revolution'.

Far from being the source of all conflicts and an obstacle to human flourishing, the metaphysics of religion are a necessary corrective to the shallow philosophies that reduce humans to an accidental by-product of evolutionary genetic biology, or that consign us to meaningless existentialism that we seek to self-medicate through 'retail therapy' and where the person who dies with the most toys wins. Wins what exactly?

No, religion is not to blame. In an increasingly fearful world, attributed to the randomness of chance, the victory of the strongest and the apparent meaninglessness of death, the world's religions, informed by reason, can rightly point to deeper truths and assure us: 'Be not afraid!'

3. The Buddhist tradition
ADDRESS BY HIS HOLINESS THE DALAI LAMA

Respected spiritual brothers, sisters and also other brothers and sisters, I am indeed very, very happy to participate in this meaningful inter-faith dialogue. All the speakers representing the theistic traditions gave really wonderful presentations, so I very much appreciate it.

For my part, I think all points of importance have been addressed so there is nothing left! You—Alex and I—are representative of non-theistic religions; that is Buddhism and also Jainism, and another ancient Indian form of religious tradition that we call Sankya tradition. Within this Sankya tradition, there are two groups—one that accepts a creator God and one that does not. So these three—that part of Sankya tradition, the Jain tradition and the Buddhist tradition—seem to be the major non-theistic religious traditions.

So there are big differences between these traditions in terms of absolute truth or ultimate truth. In the theistic tradition, absolute reality or ultimate truth is God or creator. And from that theistic perspective, there are beautiful reasons for seeing that God is full of compassion or full of love. We come from such a source.

One time I asked my Christian brother: 'What does it matter whether you accept the notion of previous life or rebirth?' He told me that Christianity has no idea about previous life because this very life is created by God. So when I heard this explanation, I really felt: 'Oh that's a really, really very powerful presentation. This very life created by God.' So we ourselves have a direct link to our creator, so the sense of intimacy with God can become very, very powerful. So there is greater possibility to listen to God's wishes and message because we have such a close feeling.

All three speakers emphasise that we should extend love to all creatures because we are all from the same source.

But Buddhists are non-theistic, so then how do Buddhists advise that you should be a warm-hearted person? Here we have a different approach. But in all Buddhist texts and in all Jain texts, the message of the Buddha, the message of Mahavira, all carry the same message—that of love, compassion, tolerance, forgiveness.

So philosophically, we may be different, but fundamentally it's the same practice, the same message. So far as Buddhism is concerned, the Buddhist reason in order to be a compassionate person, all phenomena that are momentarily changing is due to its own causes and conditions.

So therefore, pleasure and pain are also due to their own causes and conditions. Pain and pleasure are not themselves something independent, but arise due to their own causes and conditions.

Therefore since we want happiness and joyfulness, we must take care about the causes and conditions of these things. Since we don't want pain and trouble, we have to look very seriously at the possible causes and conditions of pain and suffering.

So having identified that an action creates pain for others, then that becomes the cause for one's own pain. The compassionate action to serve and help others, that action creates happiness and a happy experience to arise. So these consequences arise later as benefit to self, as pleasure happiness.

So on the basis of the law of causality, the non-theistic religious traditions emphasise that you should not harm others. You should if possible help others, if not, at least, resist harming others. That's the Buddhist explanation.

Now look at the practices—they are the same: love, compassion, resisting harming one another.

So the next question is: 'Why do we have these different approaches?' Then the reason: the Buddha taught his followers different philosophies and particularly in the Sanskrit tradition, there were different philosophies taught by the same teacher, the Buddha.

I occasionally express, with the deepest respect for the Buddha, the contradictory philosophies taught by the same teacher is certainly not due to his own confusion. Certainly not. It's not that today he taught some philosophy, but today he forgot what he taught so today he says something different! Certainly not. Nor could the Buddha have created or intended to create more confusion amongst his followers. Certainly not.

So the question is: 'Why did he teach different philosophies?' The answer is that amongst the Buddha's followers, there were people of different mental dispositions. Therefore the same purpose, object or goal, but different methods of approach according to their different mental dispositions. He deliberately taught different philosophies or methods according to their different mental disposition, but the same purpose, the same goal.

From this fact, we can learn that in a different location, different time and different teachers taught different philosophies such as theistic religion. But it's very necessary and useful to those people in that particular area and that particular time.

So therefore, firstly, in the field of practice, there are many similarities. In fact the practices of love and compassion and forgiveness are the same. And then different philosophies have the same purpose, in order to strengthen the same basic practices. So there is no problem.

In fact we should be grateful for those ancient masters. They taught many different ways of approach to strengthen the practice of love, compassion and forgiveness in order to create a happier society, happier humanity, but to use different philosophies.

So that's one way to reduce conflict in the name of different religions and philosophies.

Then another field, if we try to develop a happy human society only through religious faith, then that would be difficult. There are six billion humans but a large portion, strictly speaking, are not believers. Many people might identify with a family connection with a religious tradition, but [in] individual cases they are not really serious. Some people might therefore recite prayers and other words, but not really believe in them or [have] much interest in them.

That's why very unhealthy things are happening in all societies. So if people who claim 'I'm a Christian' or 'I'm a Muslim' or 'I'm a Jew' and 'Buddhist or Hindu', if they truly respected their traditions and beliefs then we should not expect any problems! But there are six billion human beings, but they are full of problems!

There are always mischievous people amongst Christians, Muslims, Jews, Buddhists, Hindus and Jains. Mischievous people are always there. So we need another approach. That could be secular ethics or secular humanism.

For some reason, my Muslim friends in inter-faith dialogue suggest that secularism means rejection of religion. But according to my Indian friends, their interpretation about secularism is not rejection of religion, but respect for all religions and equal respect and treatment of all religious practitioners. This includes equal respect for non-believers.

Therefore we need a secular ethics without necessarily accepting some belief or faith. I find that now some scientists, especially the neuroscientists, say that a compassionate mind is very good for our immune system and that anger is actually eating our immune system.

One day in Japan, during a meeting with some doctors, one doctor told me that when you are treating a patient, trust is very important. So this doctor asked me about the way to develop trust.

I responded: 'I don't know. Maybe trust comes from warm-heartedness.' A doctor may be very well qualified, but through a lack of warm-heartedness, they may treat a patient without much human feeling, like they are repairing a machine. Then it's very difficult from the patient's side to develop trust.

From my own side, when I have had treatment in hospital and have gone into machines and have had injections, when the doctors and nurses approach you without a smile then I have felt a little uncomfortable.

But then doctors and nurses come to you with some warmth, then you feel that these people will take [the] fullest care of you. So therefore in order to develop trust between doctors, nurses and patients, there is no other way than to develop a genuine concern and care—in other words, love. When I responded like this to the doctor in Japan, he seemed to agree.

There is a saying amongst Tibetans that 'such and such a person is a great physician, but their heart does not have much warmth, so sometimes the patient does not recover very quickly. But that there are doctors who are not famous, but have a warm heart, then their medicine seems to be more effective.'

I think in modern society, besides the sophisticated machines, from the doctor's side, from the nurse's side, a warm-heartedness is necessary. A realisation that others' pain is just like your own pain, then they will take the fullest care.

Every human movement ultimately depends on motivation, whether lawyer, teacher, politician, businessperson, whether their professional work becomes helpful to society or not depends entirely on their motivation.

In order to develop proper motivation, the various religious traditions have a very important role. Then those people who do not have much interest in religion, then another way, a secular way is to educate oneself as to the importance of these inner values. I think that is the way to promote human values and these good qualities.

So is religion only a source of trouble? Certainly not. I mentioned earlier that there will always be mischievous people in all religions. There are two categories. One category of these people is not religiously minded. Their interest is in power for political or economic reasons and they manipulate religion to gain it. That is understandable.

Then another category [is] sincere believers and practitioners. We cannot describe such people as mischievous people. I think they are very sincere. But the concept of one truth, one religion becomes a problem. In ancient times, practitioners believed their religion had the one truth. They believed other religions were wrong. Because of that kind of belief, conversions by force in the past were common.

But today, in the twenty-first century, every part of the world is connected through information and economies and tourism. We are very much intermixed. For this reason, such attitudes are lessening. But we still need many more occasions for inter-religious dialogue and meeting people.

For myself, since 1975, I have practised four methods in order to develop religious harmony.

1. Meeting scholars from different traditions and discussing similarities and differences in approach. When differences arise, we discuss where they come from and what is their purpose.
2. Meeting people from different traditions who are not necessarily scholars but to exchange their deeper spiritual experiences. This really helps to realise the value of other traditions. From my own side, I met the late Thomas Merton and Mother Teresa and other Catholic monks and nuns. As a result of meeting such practitioners, I really developed a genuine respect and admiration for how much they contribute to human society.
3. Going on pilgrimage to different holy places. Since 1975, I started this practice at Sarnath in India. There are Christian churches and Jain, Buddhist and Hindu temples are there (with the exception of a Jewish synagogue). One day I made a pilgrimage to them. Since then I go to these sacred places and pay homage. With this spirit of pilgrimage, I visited Jerusalem twice. We started with prayer at the Western Wall, then went to an ancient Christian church and then to a mosque. At first, myself and some Jewish friends went. Then the second time, some Hindu and Muslim friends went. One time, in India at Bodhgaya—the most sacred place, where Buddha Shakyamuni attained enlightenment—some Christian friends from England joined me in three days' dialogue at Bodhgaya. For 20 minutes each morning, every morning, we meditated together in silence under the bodhi tree. We were Buddhist and Christian brothers and sisters as well as some Muslims and Hindus, meditating together. These sorts of meetings are very important and very powerful in developing a certain vibration. You can feel a certain vibration. When I visited Lourdes and Fatima, I could feel something very wonderful.
4. Leaders of different traditions come together like the meeting at Assisi and speak the same message of love, of compassion and peace.

So in conclusion, we still need to promote these kinds of messages. That way, the concept of one religion and one truth may loosen up. In individual cases, the concept of one truth and religion is very important. I am Buddhist and in practice, one tradition, truth and reality in the form of Buddhist teaching is very important.

For my Christian and Jewish friends, the Christian or Jewish tradition is the only truth, the only religion. But whether we accept it or not, there is in society many different views, a multi-religious faith system—that is fact. But there is no contradiction because for the individual there is one truth and religion and this is very necessary. And in groups of people, in society, there are many different views and several different religions. That is fact.

We should therefore be realistic and accept this reality. If we do accept this reality then there will be no problem. Thank you!

4. The Catholic tradition
ADDRESS BY MOST REVEREND CHRISTOPHER PROWSE, CATHOLIC AUXILIARY BISHOP OF MELBOURNE

Global friendship

What an honour it is for me to represent the Christian faith at this inter-faith dialogue, One World—Many Paths to Peace, in the presence of His Holiness the Dalai Lama. We are so honoured by your presence with us, Your Holiness.

I am a Catholic bishop. I understand that over the years you have had dialogue with many Catholic leaders—in fact, no less than with three popes and several well-known Catholic monks, including Thomas Merton and Laurence Freeman. You have become a real pioneer of peace making between our two different traditions. You are willing to meet with us, to talk with us, to learn from each other. For this we are so grateful.

You understand well that these encounters are new to both Buddhists and Christians. I believe that these encounters are forging a fruitful friendship between the both of us. Friendship is surely the ultimate answer to the misuse of religion as a false pretext for war and terror. If the perception is that religion only causes world problems and creates enemies, then friendship between us is an urgent priority.

But friendship cannot be forced upon anyone. There first must be a willingness to be friends.

For Catholics, this willingness has been expressed in more recent decades. Our Vatican II Council (1962–1965) opened the door to such dialogue when it stated that

> Buddhism in its various forms testifies to the essential inadequacy of this changing world. It proposes a way of life by which men can, with confidence and trust, attain a state of perfect liberation and reach perfect illumination either through their own efforts or by the aid of divine help. (*Nostra Aetate* 1965:n. 2)

So our willingness for friendship has been established. This is a great achievement in our times. Where do we go from here? How can different faiths deepen friendship so that the one world of peace may flourish?

May I offer humbly a suggestion? It has three parts (I am indebted to Father Patrick O'Sullivan sj for this expression):

- when power meets power, there is a power struggle
- when power meets vulnerability, there is alienation
- when vulnerability meets vulnerability, there is intimacy.

History is replete with examples of power struggles arising from individuals or communities, even religious communities, refusing to give way or make room for each other.

Likewise, the alienation of vulnerable peoples when they meet the force of an advancing power can be devastating. For example, our own Australian Aboriginal and Torres Strait Islanders are witnesses to this. But when vulnerability in the human heart meets the vulnerability of another, the intimacy of a strong and constant friendship has a chance of growing. It is like a little seed that might just grow as tall and strong as a mighty Australian gum tree.

It is this latter type of encounter between us that may enable a friendship to grow that is worthy of our common humanity. It is a shared vulnerability that becomes a fertile soil enabling peace to grow and the flowers of mutual respect to bloom.

Are we strong enough to be vulnerable to each other?

Let me explain from a Christian point of view.

For us, friendship based on vulnerability is not sentimental or individualistic. It is strong and arises from the dignity of the human person who is made in the image and likeness of God. The foundation of all human rights arises from this union of the creator with the created. This type of friendship with God and each other condemns outright caricatures of itself as a reason for war or terrorist acts. It embraces the common good. Friendship is motivated by compassion. It works towards a global peace ethic based on solidarity with each other.

It is ready to see 'the other' not as a threat but as a brother or sister who 'completes' me. It desires that the poor and marginalised come into the centre of the circle of life. It is ready to forgive and show mercy. It acknowledges the beauty of all creation and strives to respect it.

Christians believe that the greatest form of vulnerability ever shown was the death of Jesus of Nazareth. The crucified Jesus is our living symbol of the divine vulnerability that our loving and merciful God was prepared to make for us by sending His only Son, Jesus Christ, to die for us. Jesus gave himself up for us all. He took on all our vulnerabilities and weaknesses in everything, except sin. In profound humility, Jesus became for all time the 'Lamb of God who takes away the sins of the world'.

In the Resurrection of Jesus Christ, our Lord and Saviour, and by the sending of His Holy Spirit upon us, true intimacy with God has been established. This is our Good News. Together with all religions and all men and women of goodwill, Christians desire to build continuously a culture of peace. This is the fruit of true friendship and it dispels the midnight of war and welcomes the dawn of peace.

This friendship is a work of justice. It builds and restores damaged or broken relationships with God, humans and the Earth. It is a permanent task. It is the fruit of love. Its soul is compassion and mercy.

Given the fragile nature of the world today, global friendship is the medicine so badly needed. It is almost as if—please excuse this strange expression—we are 'condemned' to friendship. Alternatives seem unthinkable. Buddhists and Christians, Muslims and Jews are well placed to continue to offer leadership in global friendship. Loving kindness is surely at the heart of all our religious traditions.

I conclude by offering a beautiful story that I believe originates from ancient Jewish texts. Understandably, over time, many variations have arisen but this is the version that I have received. It is a story of a Jewish teacher who asks his students how they can tell when the night has gone and the dawn has arrived. One student suggests it is when you can look out and a person can be distinguished from a dog. Another suggests it is when you can look out and distinguish the difference between a house and a tree. But the theologian's response was that the night has gone and the dawn has arrived when you can look into the eyes of another and say: 'You are my brother; you are my sister.'

Your Holiness the Dalai Lama and Rabbi Jonathan Keren-Black and Professor Abdullah Saeed, I look at you today with eyes of loving kindness and I say: You are my dear brothers. Let us go forward together!

5. The Jewish tradition
ADDRESS BY RABBI JONATHAN KEREN-BLACK

A Jewish understanding

The orthodox Chief Rabbi of Great Britain and the Commonwealth, Dr Jonathan Sacks, illustrates the cover of his remarkable book *Dignity of Difference* with a picture of the Tower of Babel.

The straightforward meaning of the Babel story (Genesis Chapter 11:1–9) is well known—that the peoples of the Earth tried to build a tower to place themselves in the heavens and replace God, and that God subverted their plans by making them speak different languages so that they could no longer communicate, leaving no choice but to go their different ways.

Rabbi Sacks adds a completely new and positive meaning to the story. This is the episode, he suggests, where God creates different languages, different cultures and different experiences of God—ultimately, different religions. In his reading, we are all equally God's children—and this of course we find often through Jewish writings—but crucially, Rabbi Sacks implies, we also all share parts of the truth.

Let me go even further and say that the people's original intent may have been to build an edifice to 'make a name for themselves' (Genesis 11:4) (or did they really mean to replace and overthrow God?), but the denouement of the story was that they were scattered over the face of the Earth (Genesis 11:9). Today, what can be more pressing than to gather together again to work for the common good—no less than survival? At the point in history where we have the dreadful and proven capacity to destroy each other en masse, as well as the challenges to survival that we human beings have brought to our environment, let us bring together our many and varied understandings and insights of the millennia since Babel. Together let us acknowledge that there is indeed an ultimate power and wisdom that all humanity senses and seeks, but that it is greater than all of us, and cannot be encapsulated or claimed by any one religion; that we must either work together or face the dark consequences.

The sins of scripture

To me, it seems there is no point in denying the difficulties in our texts—what the insightful Episcopalian Bishop John Shelby Spong calls 'the sins of scripture'. Over 4000 years of tradition and experience—when often those around us wanted us destroyed and indeed our memory and our God obliterated—it would be highly surprising if there were none. What is more instructive is to look at what we are taught, consistently and systematically as our tradition develops and matures, to see what we teach our children, and indeed what we try to do.

Peace seeking but not pacifist

Judaism seeks peace as a precious and important commodity. The Hebrew Bible instructs us to seek peace and pursue it (Psalm 34:15). In the prophet Isaiah's messianic vision, 'nation shall not lift up sword against nation, neither shall they learn war anymore' (Isaiah 2:4). This is not of course the same as being pacifist, however. There are times when we must stand up for our belief, our God, our freedom—even at the cost of our lives.

When I hear the laudable aims of passive resistance, of non-violent teachings, as a Jew, I am immediately faced with two historical truths: six million of my people had effectively no choice but non-violent resistance, with terrible and tragic results beyond our comprehension. And, when, under United Nations agreement, the State of Israel was declared in 1948, it was immediately attacked by the five surrounding countries, and, had it not been able to respond by armed force, it would have been overrun and destroyed in little more than the three minutes it takes to fly from one side of it to the other. And this is without exploring the threat of the many other murderous dictatorships of history, and what would have happened had we relied on passive resistance at those times.

Rabbinic writings from nearly 2000 years ago repeatedly highlight the value of peace. For example: 'In God's eyes, the person stands high who makes peace between people—between husband and wife, between parents and children, between management and labour, between neighbour and neighbour. But the one who establishes peace among the nations stands highest of all.' 'Work for peace in your home, then in your street, then in your city,' we are instructed. Work *'mipnei darkhei shalom'*—for the sake of peace. According to Rabbi Simeon ben Gamliel, three things preserve the world: truth, justice and peace (Avot 1:18).

Contemporary response

To know the way that a religion today responds to the needs and issues of our time, we have to locate and listen to the leading voices who know and understand our own context, and interpret and teach it for us, 'standing on the shoulders' of those who have gone before. Rabbi Sacks stands out, deeply rooted as he is both in the Jewish and the Western traditions. The message of peace and shared understanding is common within progressive Jewish leadership, but I quote Rabbi Sacks exactly because he is a spokesperson for the more traditional orthodox, albeit 'modern orthodox', part of our spectrum.

In his 2005 book, *To Heal a Fractured World*, he writes 'too often [religion] appears on the news, and lodges in the mind, as extremism, violence and aggression'. But, he goes on to emphasise his previous message: 'goodness and virtue are widely distributed through humanity.'

'Many times,' he writes:

> I have been inspired by the community-building, life-transforming, hope-creating work of Christians, Muslims, Hindus, Sikhs, Buddhists, Jains, Zoroastrians, Baha'i; indeed of every faith with whom it has been my privilege to come into contact. Equally I value the moral force of many forms of secular humanism, from John Stuart Mill to Bertrand Russell and beyond.

Inter-faith messages

It is on the firm Jewish basis of developing a world of understanding and respect for difference and diversity that my inter-faith work over the past several years has involved developing a project which takes a Jew, a Christian and a Muslim into secondary schools, where they deliver the message that *every* faith has value, and that indeed we all share many important values. An important aspect of the message is non-verbal—the three presenters are modelling that they are friends, that they work together, respect each other and listen to each other, and to the students, with care and empathy, and seek to understand.

To commence each workshop, we devised a short film. It starts by showing the Milky Way, then cuts to the familiar image of the Earth in the darkness of space, stating that 'in the magnitude of the cosmos…we all share a small planet. What happens in one part of the world can affect us all. Pollution, poverty, industrialisation, urbanisation.' How well we now, albeit belatedly, realise this! 'It's the same with religions', the film continues. We then come to our first vox-pop—a group of teenagers tells us what they think is bad about religions.

We start there because our experience is that, sadly, too many young people—and the not so young as well—believe religion is indeed the cause of many of the world's problems. The film journeys on, giving the teenagers the opportunity to state some good things about religion as well, and ultimately to pose the questions they would ask religious leaders. 'Why must you fight? Why can't we all get along? Why can't you get your religious messages across?' Well, to those of you reading this piece, I now convey their simple, crucial questions.

I am delighted to report that these workshops have been really well received and the questions the students raise have been excellent; by going into the schools with this carefully constructed and professional presentation, we have moved religion from something that the students often see as boring and irrelevant, to a subject that is interesting—and even 'cool'! To emphasise interest in the beliefs and practices of others, to develop respect for difference and diversity, and all for only $10 per student seems to me to be a pretty good investment in the future! The schools who have had it agree, and manage to find the funding to bring it back each year. It is a wonderful and effective project, ready to roll out across Australia if we could find the funding to develop the structure and support it!

Not just three faiths

Of course, Jews, Christians and Muslims share a great deal in common: texts, stories, characters, history as well as common values and underpinned by an ethical monotheistic approach. Yet we live in a richly multi-faith and multicultural society; it is estimated that there are more than 120 religious approaches within Victoria alone. Therefore we have recently tried a new structure—a group determined by various approaches to a common issue or set of issues. This is how GreenFaith Australia came about—a rich and diverse group of people whose faith compels them to engage in environmental and ecological concerns for the sake of understanding, education, improvement, for the sake of peace.

Equal but different

As I have said, Judaism is suffused with a strong wish, a powerful drive, for peace. Of course, we are not alone in this. The problems arise in society when we think that everyone else should be like us. I believe that Judaism never really suffered from this mentality, as it has always maintained that there are multiple paths to God and to salvation at the end of days—whatever 'the end of days' may mean! You don't have to be Jewish—you are only required to be a decent human being—to observe what are known as the 'Noahide laws' (derived from Noah).

Jews, it is said, have 613 commandments to obey, but for everyone else there are only seven Noahide ones—things like not murdering, ensuring an accessible system of justice in your community, and prohibiting the tearing of limbs from living animals. Observe them and you get exactly the same 'reward' in the end!

We find, from the very start of Genesis, a pre-modern version of equality as well: when God created humanity—not Adam as usually translated, but A-Dam, humanity—God created them equal, male and female at the same moment, and every one in God's image (Genesis, 1:27). Every one. Clearly, that means all of humanity—men, women, red, brown, white, yellow, purple, big, small, even regardless of their sexuality—every single one in God's image. Today we understand, perhaps more clearly than our ancestors in years past, that you are what you are—be it woman or man, black skinned or white, heterosexual or homosexual or somewhere in between. And what we are—what every single human being is—is an image of God.

Therefore we must surely use our gift of wisdom to extend our care and compassion, our love and support and acceptance, to every human being in need. This would be a position of moral high ground to which we should hope and encourage every human being to climb.

Many paths to peace

'Come ye,' calls the prophet Isaiah through the millennia, 'let us go up to the mountain of God, that we should learn of God's ways, and walk in God's paths' (Isaiah 2:3–5). Paths, let us note, and not one single path. From this, we can certainly call on the powerful image that there are many paths up the mountain. As they get further up, the paths may run alongside each other and sometimes cross, but must inevitably converge, until ultimately they all reach the same goal—not that in the story of the Tower of Babel of aggrandisement and perhaps overthrowing God, but of achieving their full human potential.

That goal may have many names: communion with God, nirvana, salvation, redemption, eternal life. Surely, ultimately, whatever else it may be for travellers on the various steep paths, it truly is the same thing—it is *shalom, salam*—it is true peace. May all our steps lead us towards it.

6. The Islamic tradition
ADDRESS BY PROFESSOR ABDULLAH SAEED

Your Holiness, friends, brothers and sisters. A very good afternoon to you, and *Assalamu alaykum*, meaning, 'Peace be with you'.

It is a great pleasure to be here to share with so many people this magnificent ceremony to honour such a distinguished and well-loved man of peace.

As a Muslim, it is my belief that Islam, like all other religions, holds as its core value a fundamental commitment to peace. To this end, Islam has quite a lot of resources to support and promote peace.

These resources range from scripture, to historical narratives, to ethical and moral values, and the very big ideas and values that occupy the thinking of most of us today.

The foundation for peace in Islam is based on four basic ideas.

First, all human beings of all ethnicities and languages are part of one family, with one father and mother.

Second, the One God, the Creator and Sustainer of the Universe, does not want all people to be carbon copies of one another; differences in religion, language, colour, race are very much part of God's plan.

Third, God provided guidance to all people on Earth, not just a select few, and based on that Islam recognises and respects prophets, teachers, scriptures and teachings that came before Prophet Muhammad.

Fourth, human beings are commanded to conduct their affairs based on fairness, justice and equity and to reject all forms of injustice and oppression.

I could quote a wealth of texts from the holy scripture of Islam and precedents from Muslim history to provide support for the idea of the importance of peace.

Let me give a couple of examples.

The holy scripture of Islam says that God loves those who deal with other people on the basis of kindness, fairness and justice; that God loves those who do good deeds; that Muslims should seek the path of peace, not violence and injustice.

This is not just for the human beings; it is for all living beings. The Prophet Muhammad once said that a person who let a cat starve to death will be punished for that.

Now, let me mention a few things from a Muslim's day-to-day life that keeps peace at the forefront of a Muslim's mind.

For example, the most common greeting among Muslims is '*assalamu alaykum*', which means 'peace be with you'. This greeting is repeated by Muslims hundreds of millions of times every day right across the globe.

Another example is: when a Muslim begins to do anything, even very mundane things, usually he or she will say, in Arabic, 'I begin this in the name of God, the Most Compassionate, the Most Merciful'. Again, a statement made hundreds of millions of times a day.

The key attribute of the God Muslims worship is compassion and mercy. More importantly, one of the names of God is 'Peace' or the 'Giver of Peace'.

The Prophet Muhammad once said a Muslim is not a Muslim until he or she stops harming others. A Muslim is commanded not to kill a human being. One Qur'anic verse says that killing one human being is equivalent to killing the entire humanity.

This respect is for all human beings. Once the Prophet Muhammad was sitting with some of his followers and he saw a funeral procession of a Jewish person passing. He stood up as a mark of respect. His followers asked him why he stood up for a non-Muslim. He replied: because he is a human being, like any other.

But you may ask, if this is the Islam that Muslims follow, why is there so much hatred, killing, maiming, bombing and destruction today in the name of Islam?

The answer is not so simple. But let me try.

First, Muslims, 1300 million of them, do not function, behave and do things exactly in the same way. There are many differences among Muslims about what Islam means and how a Muslim should interpret the scripture and tradition. Most Muslims would be quite comfortable with what I have said about Islam and peace. But there are some Muslims who do not share that view.

Second, Islam and its history and traditions as well as Muslim practice in the past could be likened to a garden—a garden with beautiful flowers, splendid colours and wonderful trees. But the garden also has hidden beneath this beauty some ugly aspects: dead trees, weeds, thorns and the like.

Most Muslims emphasise the beauty of their religion and its traditions; some Muslims ignore the beauty and emphasise the ugly bits. Some forms of violence were part of these ugly bits in Muslim history.

How do most Muslims handle some of the ugly bits from their past practice and tradition? This is largely through reinterpretation.

Like any other religion, Islam is going through a process of adjusting to the changing needs and circumstances of today.

Today

- we live in a world that is interconnected
- we emphasise quite a lot human rights
- we emphasise the need for all religious traditions to get together and engage in inter-faith dialogue
- we are talking about creating a culture of peace
- we are all concerned about the impact of what we do on the fragile planet.

These ideas and values are part of most religious traditions, including Islam. These big ideas and values shape the thinking of most Muslims today.

Muslims often reinterpret those parts of their history, practice and tradition that go against these big ideas and values. Those parts that are in conflict with these big ideas and values are marginalised and forgotten.

Peace is one such big idea. It always has been. Today, its importance is far greater than at any other time in history. Muslims, like others, have to draw on all the resources of their faith to push for the peace project for the sake of all humanity.

This magnificent gathering here today is a superb expression of our collective commitment to peace.

Finally, peace be with you all.

7. Are religions to blame?
VENERABLE ALEX BRUCE

I'm free to do what I want any old time
I'm free to choose what I please any old time

— The Rolling Stones[1]

Introduction

Are religions to blame for the apparently endless troubles in the world? Critics point to the witness of history, claiming that the Inquisition, witch-hunts, the Crusades and civil wars demonstrate the inherent destructiveness of religion. Nations have invoked God in aid of their wars against other nations, whose inhabitants have also invoked God's protection—presumably while God cherished the peoples of both nations equally.

At best, an inadequate or naive understanding of one's own religion and the beliefs of others has resulted in 'fundamentalist' or religious extremists cheerfully assigning whole portions of the world's population to hell because they do not express the same beliefs as themselves. It has led to arrogant and confrontational 'missionary' campaigns that are considered necessary to 'save the souls' of unbelievers.

And at worst, those extremists have actively assisted the 'unbelievers' on their way through terror campaigns and suicide bombings.

In the twenty-first century, the world's religious traditions exist in largely liberal, democratic societies. Does religion have a role to play in the development of democratic societies or are religious traditions unreliable participants in the processes of democratic societies? Can liberal democratic societies really function without religious values or is all religion simply superstitious nonsense that hinders the flourishing of genuine human societies?

What does history tell us about those societies that have aggressively pursued social agendas without reference to religious values? Have they in fact resulted in more humane, more tolerant and more enlightened societies? What do the

---

1 *I'm Free,* from *The London Years* collection.

world's religions have to say about 'democracy' and what it means to create a society that places human dignity at its centre? Can the world's religions be trusted participants in the development of democratic societies around the world? Can contemporary liberal democratic societies sustain their dedication to human rights and dignity without the metaphysics underlying religion?

The presentations by His Holiness the Dalai Lama and the other representatives of the world's spiritual traditions who spoke at the 2007 One World—Many Paths to Peace Symposium argued prophetically that religious values and their underlying metaphysics did indeed have a much needed role to play in preserving the very meaning of what it was to be human, living in dignity with society.

In this chapter, I want to explore the criticisms of religion and religious values offered by contemporary, liberal democratic societies. I will explain (as best I can) how the philosophical structure of these criticisms stems from the more fundamental philosophical origins of our contemporary liberal democratic societies in the thoughts and writings of Francis Bacon, René Descartes, John Stuart Mill, Thomas Hobbes and John Locke.

I suggest that these philosophical foundations provided fertile ground for the later development of the 'atheistic humanism' established by Auguste Comte, Ludwig Feuerbach, Karl Marx and Friedrich Nietzsche, whose common foundation was an explicit rejection of the Christian God. These thinkers argued that 'shrugging off' the superstitious cloak of religion would herald a new dawn of human dignity and tolerance, in which liberal democratic societies would be characterised by the rule of reason and the annihilation of all dark and aggressive instincts.

I will suggest that instead the determined attempts to annihilate religion and religious metaphysics in society gestated the rise of nationalism, ethnocentrism and imperialism that resulted in both world wars. I will suggest that the oceans of blood and mountains of corpses that characterised much of the twentieth century were not the result of religion, but of the absence of religious metaphysics underpinning the idea of what it meant to be human in a flourishing society.

I will then move on to look at the role of religion in contemporary democratic society. Can religion and the Church be trusted to participate? Because my theological training relates to the Catholic Christian Church, I will discuss the role of the Catholic Church in general and the philosophical thought of the late Pope John Paul II in particular in exploring this issue.

I will argue that the world's religions do not pose a threat to democratic societies and in fact have a prophetic role to play in drawing attention to the limitations inherent in democratic societies. In particular, I want to suggest that there is a fundamental but relatively unexplored link between the truth of religious metaphysics and the fundamental freedoms we take for granted in democratic societies.

In the process, I hope to challenge, provoke and perhaps upset many entrenched ideas about the nature of religion and religious values and the role they can play in ensuring a free, virtuous society in which humans can flourish in dignity and peace. Above all, I will be happy if the contents of this chapter encourage respectful debate and deeper thinking!

Religion and the development of societies

Our modern liberal democratic societies did not spring into existence overnight. The society in which we live in the twenty-first century is the outcome of centuries of social experimentation, revolution and reformation.

What we call 'modernity' or the 'modern world view' had it origins in the scientific and philosophical advances in the sixteenth and seventeenth centuries. This era was thought to be 'the great formative era of modern philosophy, marked by the decline of medieval conceptions of knowledge and by the rise of the physical sciences'.[2]

With the 'scientific revolution' ignited by Copernicus, Newton, Kepler and Galileo, an explanation for the movement of the heavens was no longer to be found in the ancient Aristotelian and Ptolemaic insistence on perfect spheres and circles.[3] Rather, the Sun, Earth and the stars were subject to mathematical scrutiny and were found to move according to reasoned and tested physical principles. So

> [b]etween the fifteenth and seventeenth centuries, the West saw the emergence of a newly self-conscious and autonomous human being— curious about the world, confident in his own judgements, sceptical of orthodoxies, rebellious against authority, responsible for his own beliefs and actions, enamoured of the classical past but even more committed to a greater future, proud of his humanity, conscious of his distinctness from nature, aware of his artistic powers as individual creator, assured of his intellectual capacity to comprehend and control nature, and altogether less dependent on an omnipotent God.[4]

---

2 Hampshire, S. 1956, *The Age of Reason,* Mentor Books, United Kingdom, p. 1.
3 Contrary to popular belief, Copernicus was never persecuted by the Catholic Church and even dedicated his seminal text *de Revolutionibus* to the Pope.
4 Tarnas, R. 1999, *The Passion of the Western Mind,* Pimlico, United Kingdom, p. 282.

The use of reason rather than blind belief, the self-confidence in mastery over mind and nature influenced the subsequent philosophical revolution. The focus of this revolution was on the autonomous individual subject as the determinant of conduct.

Francis Bacon

Francis Bacon criticised the *deductive* methodology of acquiring knowledge as being overly dependent on presuppositions that could not be empirically verified. For Bacon, the human mind was to observe, measure and evaluate objective events and, from those empirical observations, draw conclusions about what could be known.

This movement from the general to the particular was a use of *inductive* reasoning that did not depend on *a priori* assumptions to which observed and scientifically measured phenomena had to conform.

There was no room for religious metaphysics in Bacon's approach to 'life, the universe and everything'. Bacon was one of the first 'empirical rationalists' or 'scientific empiricists', insisting that what mattered was what could be assessed scientifically and exploited pragmatically. Bacon was 'one of the first to see that scientific knowledge could give man power over nature, and therefore that the advance of science could be used to promote human plans and prosperity on an unimaginable scale'.[5]

Bacon's views also implied a distinction between 'being' and 'meaning'. The meaning of an object was not to be found in something inherent to the object, but rather in what the *subject* (the observer or user of the object) ascertained that meaning to be. An object had no intrinsic value simply because it existed (being); the value or usefulness of that object depended on personal or social preference.

René Descartes

It was René Descartes' famous statement *'cogito ergo sum'* ('I think therefore I am') that placed the person squarely as the referent for the basis of meaning and value. Descartes' formulation—placing the thinking subject at the centre of meaning—carries with it the consequence that the autonomous individual becomes the ground of knowledge, of what is true.

---

5   Magee, B. 1998, *The History of Philosophy*, Dorling Kindersley, United Kingdom, p. 75.

Descartes' views establish the foundations of *subjective* (or *individual*) *relativism* in which 'what is true for you is true for you, and what is true for me is true for me, provided we don't hurt each other'. The value or truth of an object is thus determined by subjective preference and pragmatism—what 'I' want.[6]

John Stuart Mill

The idea that 'what is true for you is true for you, and what is true for me is true for me, provided we don't hurt each other' also owes much of its force to John Stuart Mill. With Martin Luther, Mill shared a childhood dominated by an impossibly demanding father. Ultimately, Mill suffered a breakdown at the tender age of twenty. Mill's famous work *On Liberty*[7] contains the famous dictum: 'The only freedom which deserves the name is that of preserving our own good in our own way, so long as we do not attempt to deprive others of theirs, or impede their efforts to attain it.'[8]

In contemporary liberal democracies, Mill's idea of freedom has been interpreted to mean 'moral neutrality'. On this view, democratic governments should not try to form the character of their citizens, nor should those governments legislate or encourage any particular idea of what it means to be a 'virtuous' human. Rather, governments should provide a form of a 'neutral framework' of rights within which people can choose their own ends.[9]

Thomas Hobbes

What people are choosing is to accumulate, consume and enjoy pleasure. Thomas Hobbes contributed to this view in suggesting that society and politics should be structured primarily in terms of the individual's concern with material prosperity and comfortable self-preservation. Hobbes had a fairly dim view of the human capacity for exercising choice to pursue higher goals. Hobbes thought that what lay at the heart of humanity was a restless search for power in order to satisfy needs and desires. Writing in his *Leviathan*, Hobbes believes that

> felicity of this life consists not in the repose of a mind satisfied, for there is no such *finis ultimus* (utmost aim) nor *summum bonum* (greatest good) as is spoken of in the Books of the old Moral Philosophers. Felicity is a continual progress of the desire, from one object to another; the

---

6 Tilley, R. 2007, *Benedict XVI and the Search for Truth*, St Paul's Publications, Australia, p. 49.
7 Published in 1859 with the help of his wife, Harriet Taylor, whom Mill had met and formed a passionate relationship with while Taylor was married to someone else.
8 Mill, J. S. 1954, *On Liberty*, Oxford University Press, Oxford, p. 18.
9 Sandel, M. 1996, 'America's search for a new public philosophy', *Atlantic Monthly* (January), pp. 54–7.

attaining of the former being still but the way to the later. [Man seeks to] assure forever the way of his future desire; a general inclination of all mankind, a perpetual and restless desire of power after power that ceases only in death.[10]

According to Hobbes, humans are fundamentally self-interested creatures 'seeking their own benefit and promotion'. The continual struggle of humans competing against humans in the exercise of power to acquire limited resources and the fear of losing them is one of the causes of warfare.

It is difficult not to draw the conclusion that Hobbes was right; contemporary society does seem to be made up of 'they whom necessity or covetousness keep focussed on their trades and labour, and they on the other side, whom superfluity or sloth carries after their sensual pleasures'. One of my favourite authors, Felipe Fernandez-Armesto, noted, in his characteristically caustic manner, this Hobbesian tendency in today's affluent Western societies:

> The leisure conferred by prosperity in the modern West is more likely to be spent in trash-entertainments, mindless self-indulgence and festeringly slobbish indulgence than in serious meditation about life, death and the cosmos. In the pockets of most people, money buys a life of sensation, not of thought.[11]

John Locke

The transition from these individualised ways of thinking to the political organisation of society owed much to John Locke, an Englishman who was associated with the 'Glorious Revolution' of 1688 and whose writing, in turn, influenced the philosophical foundations of the French and American Revolutions.

Locke was an *empiricist*, believing that we came to know something only through our senses interacting with external stimuli. Locke therefore believed that our understanding of the world was derivative; it came from what our sense could perceive. Everything else is beyond our capacity to know. People are like blank slates, coming into the world without knowledge and gradually acquiring knowledge of the world through contact with external phenomena. And even then, that knowledge can be only a working possibility because our experience of it can be subject to error.

---

10   Hobbes, T. 1991, *Leviathan*, Oxford University Press, Oxford, p. 70.
11   Fernandez-Armesto, F. 1997, *The Future of Religion*, Phoenix, United Kingdom, p. 39.

When the American 'founding fathers' drafted the US Constitution, they specifically referred to Locke in their correspondence with each other.[12] Locke's theories translated easily into the political economy. Locke thought that it would be wrong for political and religious leaders to legislate their beliefs on the community since their knowledge might be susceptible to error.

This view was coupled with Locke's insistence that governments had the express duty to preserve the rights and freedoms of members of society. Tolerance of individual rights and views was a significant feature of Locke's political philosophy.

Evolution of humanity free of religion

These ways of thinking about what it means to be human and to be human within society ultimately influenced later public philosophers. Auguste Comte considered that empirical science was humanity's only reliable guide to living a good life. Ludwig Feuerbach employed subjectivism to conclude that religion generally and God specifically were nothing more than the wishful and subjected projections of humans; Karl Marx and Friedrich Nietzsche completed the gradual demise of religious metaphysics—Marx with religion as the 'opiate of the masses' and Nietzsche's 'madman' proclaiming the death of God, therefore concluding that the wilfulness or 'will to power' was the measure of what it meant to be human.[13]

It was inevitable that after this 'Golden Age' of scientific and philosophical renewal, belief in religious metaphysics and God would be considered the last superstition for humanity to overcome in order to flourish. Confident in humanity's capacity for rational, empirical and scientific thinking, retaining a belief in a metaphysical world sounded like an active hindrance to human evolution.

Catholic Christian commentator George Weigel explains the nature of this criticism: 'Still, there is something dramatically new in the modern crisis of faith: the notion that the biblical God is an enemy of human maturity and human freedom.'[14]

---

12 Magee, B. 2001, *The Story of Philosophy*, Dorling Kindersley, United Kingdom, p. 108.
13 Weigel, G. 2005, The *Cube and the Cathedral: Europe, America and politics without God*, Basic Books, United States, p. 49.
14 Weigel, G. 2002, *The Truth of Catholicism*, Perennial Publications, United States, p. 20.

For advocates of this view, the sooner we accept that the true 'reality' of our lives is nothing more than the result of random biochemical evolution in an indifferent universe, the better we will all be. For example, Scottish author Muriel Gray wrote:

> [T]he cause of all this misery, mayhem, violence, terror and ignorance is of course religion itself. For the government of a secular country such as ours to treat religion as if it had real merit instead of regarding it as a ridiculous anachronism, which education, wisdom and experience can hopefully overcome in time, is one of the most depressing developments of the 21st century.[15]

In Franz Werfel's novel *The Song of Bernadette*, a local café owner dismisses the possibility of 'miraculous' physical cures at Lourdes. He exclaims angrily:

> The organisation of nature is a relatively simple thing. Heaven is empty and rigid space dotted by some billions of sidereal systems...in the immeasurable voids between the globes of fire there was evidently no place for the so-called supernatural. On a minor satellite of one of the least of those sidereal systems there vegetates an ape-like creature called man. The notion that a male of this animal species, above all one of its wretched females, could be the image of beings who rule the universe could only be the ideology of such primitive savages as had not yet won man's first, if not also his final victory—the renunciation of wishful dreams. Not until this sad and intentional stupidity at the basis of all illusion from the immemorial emotional delusion that he and his earth were the centre of things and his mind something other than a purposeful function of matter determined by necessity, not until he resigns himself to see his life in its true colours of a physico-chemico-biological mechanism, not until then will he begin at last to be a human being instead of a semi-animal haunted by demonic dreams. This evolution toward a truly human status will inevitably issue in tolerance, the rule of reason and the annihilation of all dark and aggressive instincts.[16]

In more recent times, similar views have been repeated, with varying degrees of sophistication, by authors such as Richard Dawkins,[17] Sam Harris[18] and

---

15 Gray, M. 2005, 'Religion itself is the fount of most evil', *Scottish Sun Herald*, 24 July 2005.
16 Werfel, F. 1970, *The Song of Bernadette*, St Martins Press, New York, pp. 259–60.
17 Dawkins, R. 2006, *The God Delusion*, Black Swan, London.
18 Harris, S. 2004, *The End of Faith: Religion, terror and the future of reason*, Simon & Schuster, New York.

Christopher Hitchens,[19] who wrote that 'civilisation consists of the leaving behind of the mentality of certainty, of the mentality of holy books and the word of God'.[20]

These new prophets of atheism have, however, also been severely criticised for their reductive and simplistic understanding of religion. It is suggested they have constructed a 'straw case'—an illusion of what religion is—and then demolished that illusion. It is a simple but ultimately shallow process exposed most recently by Karen Armstrong—one of the world's leading commentators on religious affairs.[21]

So what happened?

The future of humanity, emancipated from religion, liberated by self-interest and Nietzschean will to power, didn't turn out the way it was supposed to. In fact, history has well and truly demolished Werfel's hope that the elimination of religion would result in an evolution towards a truly human status that 'will inevitably issue in tolerance, the rule of reason and the annihilation of all dark and aggressive instincts'.

The industrialised killing fields of Flanders, Ypres, the Somme, Passchendale and Gallipoli during World War I were matched in ferocity only by the Nazi blitzkrieg, the death camps of Auschwitz, Dachau and Belsen, the Russian campaign and the nuclear annihilation of Hiroshima and Nagasaki during World War II.

Recent history's 'butchers' bill' of human savagery has continued with the horrors of the Korean and Vietnam wars, the ethnic slaughter in the Balkans and in Rwanda and the 'war on terror'. Elimination of religion or religious metaphysics has not guaranteed an upward evolution in human consciousness or ethics.

It is no wonder that eminent historians such as Niall Ferguson chose titles such as *The War of the World* for their books on the history of the twentieth century.[22] Likewise, Jonathan Glover's text, which seeks to make some sense of the debasing moral history of the twentieth century, features a wounded soldier directing a massive shelling campaign.[23]

---

19   Hitchens, C. 2007, *God is Not Great: How religion poisons everything*, Twelve Books, New York.
20   Quoted in McManus, G. 2002, 'September 11: Christians blamed', *Oriens*, (Summer), <http://www.oriensjournal.com/11blamed.html>
21   Armstrong, K. 2009, *The Case for God: What religion really means*, The Bodley Head, London.
22   Ferguson, N. 2006, *The War of the World: History's age of hatred*, Allen Lane, United Kingdom.
23   Glover, J. 1999, Humanity: *A moral history of the twentieth century*, Pimlico Publishers, United Kingdom.

So pervasive did human brutality become in the twentieth century that entirely new categories of philosophical and political thought became necessary to comprehend them. For example, there is a vast literature devoted to the political and international legal implications associated with humanitarian intervention[24] and the 'responsibility to protect'.[25]

There is also exploratory literature that addresses the causes of the ethnic hatred underpinning much of the violence,[26] as well as the apparent failure of the international community, through its representative organ, the United Nations, to prevent such atrocities.[27]

The rise of atheist humanisms

Those who claim that religion is to blame for the shopping list of atrocities outlined above often ignore some harsh realities. For example, the Nazi regime's ideological focus did not stem from religious belief so much as a warped idea of nationalism that entailed the elimination of entire ethnic and religious minorities, but particularly the Jewish peoples of Europe.[28]

Likewise, Mao's 'Cultural Revolution' included the massacre of intellectuals, religious practitioners and other subversives. Stalin's and then Lenin's gulags were populated by entire groups of religious men and women. It should be remembered that a defining feature of the early to mid twentieth-century Chinese and Russian Revolutions was their determination to eradicate religion.

As I suggested above, Comte, Feuerbach, Marx and Nietzsche—whose common foundation was an explicit rejection of the Christians God—established the intellectual foundations of this way of organising society, this 'atheistic humanism'.[29]

Therefore, under the banner of 'National Socialism' or the Cultural Revolution, citizens were to be liberated from 'backward' and 'superstitious' religious metaphysics. True progress was to take place under a form of collective humanism at the direction of the State, invariably referred to as the 'Fatherland' or the 'Motherland'.[30]

---

24   Mills, N. and Brunner, K. (eds) 2002, *The New Killing Fields: Massacre and the politics of intervention*, Basic Books, New York.
25   International Commission on Intervention and State Sovereignty 2001, *The Responsibility to Protect*, December 2001,Human Security Policy Division, Human Security and Human Rights Bureau, Foreign Affairs Canada, Ottawa, Ontario.
26   Wamwere, K. 2003, *Negative Ethnicity: From bias to genocide*, Seven Stories Press, New York.
27   Traub, J. 2006, *The Best Intentions: Kofi Annan and the UN in the era of American world power*, Bloomsbury Publishing, United Kingdom.
28   Roberts, J. M. 2002, *History of the World*, (Fourth edn), Allen Lane, United Kingdom, p. 953.
29   de Lubac, H. 1949, *The Drama of Atheist Humanism*, Sheed & Ward, United Kingdom, pp. 11–12.
30   Roberts, *History of the World*, p. 1057.

The reality was, however, vastly different. The fatherlands and motherlands gestating differing forms of 'atheist humanisms' in China, Russia and Nazi Germany did not give birth to a 'golden age' of humanity liberated from superstition.

Rather, those societies most opposed to religious metaphysics—those fascist, nationalist, totalitarian or utilitarian societies—produced concentration camps, gulags, mountains of corpses and lakes of blood. Watching this orgy of self-destruction in the name of 'freedom' was French Jesuit theologian Henri de Lubac, who concluded that '[i]t is not true, as is sometimes said, that man cannot organise the world without God. What is true is that without God, he can ultimately organise it only against man. Exclusive humanism is inhuman humanism.'[31]

When religion is accused of being at the heart of the twentieth century's bloody conflicts, it is often used to 'mask' other and more immediate causes such as nationalism, ethnic hatred and imperialism. Former Secretary-General of the United Nations Kofi Annan once remarked:

> Religion is frequently equated with light. But we all know that the practice of religion can have its dark side too. Religious extremism has too often oppressed or discriminated against women and minorities. Religion has often been yoked to nationalism, stoking the flames of violent conflict and setting group against group. Religious leaders have not always spoke[n] out when their voices could have helped combat hatred and persecution or could have roused people from indifference. Religion is not itself to blame: as I have often said, the problem is usually not with the faith, but with the faithful.[32]

Is religion the enemy of 'true' democratic society?

Are religions generally and religious intervention in democratic society dangerous? The Catholic Church is a particularly active participant in democracies around the world and is frequently criticised for that participation, as if it is seeking to 'undermine democracy'.

Critics complain that by arguing for transcendental moral truths, the world's religious traditions subvert the 'freedom' underpinning liberal Western

---

31 de Lubac, *The Drama of Atheist Humanism*, p. 14.
32 Quoted in Arinze, F. 2002, *Religions for Peace*, Darton, Longman & Todd, United Kingdom, pp. 35–6.

democracies. Critics argue that 'genuine' democracy is the implementation of social policies chosen freely by a 'consensus'. For example, journalist P. P. McGuinness suggested that

> [t]he question of how far churches should play a political role is a difficult one. However, there is at least a case for demanding that churches which believe that they have a right to impose their moral preferences on the whole community should be clearly exposed as attempting to subvert democratic law-making.[33]

In 2002, at a conference in Melbourne concerning reproductive technologies, it was argued that governments should refuse to receive submissions from religious organisations because 'democracy has nothing to do with morality; it is about respecting individual choice'.[34]

The attacks against Pope John Paul II particularly—after his death in April 2005—and his views on the relationship between religious metaphysics and democracies were savage.

Homosexual activist Peter Tatchell of advocacy group OutRage! alleged that 'John Paul II waged a ceaseless war against the human rights of women and gay people, who had condemned millions to die an agonising death'.[35]

Writing in *The Guardian* newspaper on 4 April 2005, Terry Eagleton confidently declared that John Paul II's 'greatest crime' was

> [t]he grotesque irony by which the Vatican condemned as a 'culture of death' condoms, which might have saved countless lives in the developing world from an agonising AIDS death. The Pope goes to his eternal reward with those deaths on his hands. He was one of the greatest disasters for the Christian Church since Charles Darwin.[36]

Four days later and writing in the same paper, Polly Toynbee opened her assault under the tasteful title 'How dare Tony Blair genuflect on our behalf before the corpse of a man whose edicts killed millions'. Polly went on to state her belief that '[g]enuflecting before this corpse is scarcely different to parading past Lenin; they both put extreme ideology before human life and happiness at unimaginable cost'.[37]

---

33 McGuinness, P. P. 1996, 'Democracy and the right to die', *Sydney Morning Herald*, 6 July 1996.
34 Casey 2002, 'Democracy and the need for values', *The Catholic Weekly*, Sydney, 17 March 2002.
35 Quoted in 'Critics attack late Pope's views', *BBC News*, 3 April 2005, accessed 21 September 2008, <http://news.bbc.uk/go/pr/fr/-/2/hi/uk_news/4405967.stm>
36 Eagleton, T. 2005, 'The Pope has blood on his hands', *The Guardian*, 4 April 2005.
37 Toynbee, P. 2008, 'Not in my name: how dare Tony Blair genuflect on our behalf before the corpse of a man whose edicts killed millions?', *The Guardian*, 8 April 2008.

Writing in the *New Statesman* in April 2005, Michela Wrong considered that John Paul II's papacy would 'be remembered as one that helped keep Africa disease-ridden, famished and disastrously undeveloped...he did more to spread AIDS in Africa than prostitution and the trucking industry combined'.[38]

Going even further, in its 3 April edition, the *Scotland on Sunday* newspaper asked the question: 'How long before someone accuses the Pope of having committed a crime against humanity?'

What form should a sensible response to these criticisms take? To begin with, there seems to be a remarkable degree of prejudice and ignorance influencing perceptions of the value of religion and religious metaphysics.

For example, Professor Thomas Woods notes that

> [i]n our media and popular culture, little is off limits when it comes to ridiculing or parodying the Church. My own students, to the extent that they know anything at all about the Church, are typically familiar only with alleged Church 'corruption', of which they heard ceaseless tales of varying credibility from their high school teachers. The story of Catholicism, as far as they know, is one of ignorance, repression and stagnation.[39]

So virulent is this view that Pennsylvania State University's Distinguished Professor of History and Religious Studies, Philip Jenkins, has concluded that, at least in Western liberal democracies, there is 'one remaining acceptable prejudice: anti-Catholicism'.[40]

It is only recently that scholarship is recovering the crucial role that religious societies generally and the Catholic Church particularly played in the preservation and transmission of classical philosophy, mathematics and science,[41] the development of international law and free-market systems[42] and the political and intellectual development of Western societies.[43]

---

38 Wrong, M. 2005, 'The blood of innocents on his hands', *New Statesman*, 11 April 2005.
39 Woods, T. 2005, *How the Catholic Church Built Western Civilization*, Regency Publishing Inc., Washington, DC, p. 1.
40 Jenkins, P. 2003, 'Catholic-bashing: America's last acceptable prejudice', *Catalyst Magazine*, (May).
41 Rubenstein, R. 2003, *Aristotle's Children: How Christians, Muslims and Jews rediscovered ancient wisdom and illuminated the dark ages*, Harcourt Inc., United States.
42 Woods, *How the Catholic Church Built Western Civilization*.
43 Stark, R. 2005, *The Victory of Reason: How Christianity led to freedom, capitalism and Western success*, Random House, United States.

One World—Many Paths to Peace

Religion has no preference for one political system over another

Critics fail to realise, however, that the Church does not possess an inherent philosophical system of its own that it seeks to impose on society. In his 1993 encyclical *Fides et Ratio*, John Paul II pointed out:

> Underlying all the Church's thinking is the awareness that she is the bearer of a message which has its origins in God. The knowledge which the Church offers to humanity has its origin not in any speculation of her own however sublime, but in the word of God.[44]

Throughout history, the Church has drawn on existing philosophical systems to explain and proclaim that message. St Augustine drew on neo-Platonic concepts, while St Thomas Aquinas drew on Aristotelian concepts. In the late twentieth and early twenty-first centuries, John Paul II drew on the phenomenology and personalism of Max Schlerer and others.[45]

The Church also does not express an *a priori* preference for one form of political organisation or another. In his 1991 encyclical *Centesimus Annus*, John Paul II stated:

> The Church respects the legitimate autonomy of the democratic order and is not entitled to express preferences for this or that institutional or constitutional solution. Her contribution to the political order is precisely her vision of the dignity of the person revealed in all its fullness in the mystery of the Incarnate Word.[46]

Weigel explains:

> The Church is not in the business of designing or running governments; the Church is in the business of forming the kind of people who can design and run governments in which freedom leads to genuine human flourishing. From evangelism, to culture formation to political change: that is the public strategy of the Catholic Church in the twenty-first century.[47]

In expressing a preference for democracy, the Church '[v]alues the democratic system inasmuch as it ensures the participation of citizens in making political

---

44 John Paul II 1993, *Fides et Ratio*, St Paul's Publications, Sydney, p. 7.
45 Varghese, K. 2005, *Personalism in John Paul II*, Asian Trading Corporation, Bangalore, India; Kupczak, J. 2000, *Destined for Liberty: The human person in the philosophy of Karol Wojtyla/John Paul II*, The Catholic University of America Press, Washington, DC; McNerney, J. 2004, *John Paul II: Poet and philosopher*, Burns & Oates, United Kingdom.
46 John Paul II 1991, *Centesimus Annus*, Pauline Editions, Quebec, Canada, p. 47.
47 Weigel, *The Truth of Catholicism*, p. 155.

choices, guarantees to the governed the possibility both of electing and holding accountable those who govern them, and of replacing them through peaceful means when appropriate'.[48]

Democracies are not value neutral

For John Paul II and the Church, however, democracy is not a 'value-neutral' enterprise. Nor does the mere existence of a democratic system of government guarantee the freedom of its citizens; 'give me freedom or give me death' is a bluff easily called. In his address to the Bishops of Texas, Oklahoma and Arkansas during their 1998 *Ad Limina* visit, John Paul II remarked:

> [D]emocracy is itself a moral adventure, a continuing test of people's capacity to govern themselves in ways that serve the common good and the good of individual citizens. The survival of a particular democracy is imperilled when politics and law are sundered from any connection to the moral law written on the human heart.[49]

This view stands in contrast with the generally accepted understanding of democracy, embodying Mill's dictum that '[t]he only freedom which deserves the name is that of preserving our own good in our own way, so long as we do not attempt to deprive others of theirs or impede their efforts to attain it'.[50]

The 'freedom' to pursue our own good is considered value neutral; governments should not prefer or legislate for any one value system:

> The public philosophy by which we live is that freedom consists in our capacity to choose our ends for ourselves. Politics should not try to form the character or cultivate the values of its citizens. Governments should not affirm, through its policies and laws, any particular conception of the good life; it should provide a neutral framework of rights within which people can choose their own values and ends.[51]

The basis of such a value-neutral approach to democracy lies in the

> tendency to see intellectual relativism as the necessary corollary of democratic forms of political life. In such a view, truth is determined by the majority and varies in accordance with passing cultural and

---

48 Ibid., para. 46.
49 John Paul II 1999, 'Moral truth, conscience and American democracy', *The Pope Speaks*, vol. 44, no. 2 (27 June 1998), p. 96.
50 Mill, *On Liberty*.
51 Sandel, M. 1996, 'America's search for a new public philosophy', *Atlantic Monthly*, (January), p. 57.

political trends. From this point of view, those who are convinced that certain truths are absolute and immutable are considered unreasonable and unreliable.[52]

The underlying philosophical theme is that a 'true' democracy exists when a social justice issue is agreed on freely by simple consensus. These arguments are based on relativism because they appeal to simple majority views. As Cardinal Dulles argues, 'according to a widely prevalent view, [public consensus] is simply a majority opinion, which may be based on fashion or emotion, or an ideology, based on the self-interest of a class'.[53]

According to this reasoning, the 'worth' of an issue is thus determined by reference to consensus and not to transcendental moral truths for or against that issue. Markham observes that 'many imagine today that freedom is opposed to identifiable and authoritative truth. To believe in a right and wrong, which you ought to obey sounds like a prison. To believe that morality is (and should be) a matter of personal preference or opinion sounds like liberation.'[54]

Accordingly, postmodern Western democracies scorn the idea of inbuilt moral truths that are objective to society. Postmodernism regards truth as a cultural construct. I create my own truth and then express my freedom to live those truths. For the committed postmodernist and the casually cynical, Pontius Pilate's question 'Truth, what is truth?' is really the end of the debate.

The difficulty with 'I'm OK, you're OK'

The difficulty is, however, that such a view attenuates the fundamental relationship between truth and freedom in a process that descends into simple 'will to power'.

> The mere recognition that absolute truth exists provokes anxieties about an explosion of intolerance and authoritarianism and apprehension that the life of the individual will be made to conform to rigid schemes of doctrine. The contrasting poles of freedom and truth are at the root of the problems of the contemporary world. We are afraid that absolute truth will destroy and suppress human freedom, eroding our uniqueness and trying to force our highly complex world into an anachronistic fixed pattern. But if absolute truth does *not* exist, or is unrecognisable,

---

52 Pope John Paul II 2000, Democracy must be based on moral norms, Message to the Pontifical Academy of Social Sciences, 23 February 2000, para. 2.
53 Dulles, A. 1999, 'The truth about freedom: a theme from John Paul II', in J. A. DiNoia and J. A. Cessario (eds), Veritatis *Splendor and the Renewal of Moral Theology*, Scepter Publishers, Princeton, p. 139.
54 Markham, I. 1997, *Shades of grey: the Pope, Christian ethics and the ambiguity of human situations*, Trinity Papers Number 8, Trinity College, The University of Melbourne, Melbourne, Victoria, p. 8.

then even though the human attains full autonomy, all values and every distinction between good and evil lose their universal meaning. They become mere products of culture, a question of preference, of individual taste or choice.[55]

One of the consequences of this unmeasured plurality is the difficulty of achieving agreement on dramatically important ethical issues:

> North American culture…exhibits pluralism, values freedom and often accommodates moral confusion by resorting to guarantees of free choice and informed consent. Not wanting to be dogmatic or totalitarian, we edge away from difficult and divisive decisions about the morally best action or policy. Hence we find it difficult to advance toward substantive public consensus about the human good or the good society.[56]

What is needed is a recovery of dialogue between ideas of fundamental truth and human freedom. Neither should be allowed to dominate the debate. The reason why is that full autonomy on the part either of truth or freedom could easily turn into social tyranny. So if fundamentalism in truth were elevated above freedom then you might well have the ascendancy of some or other ideology that claimed fundamental rights for itself. But if absolute freedom were permitted then you might have a state of objective social anarchy.

Essentially, if there is 'my truth' and 'your truth', without any objective criteria by which to judge them, it is the most powerful party who can force its 'version' of the truth on weaker parties.[57] When this happens, a very modern form of ideological totalitarianism takes hold in which the individual is the centre of meaning and others become means to subjectively determined ends—and the people whose ends are met are the most powerful.[58]

According to the Church and John Paul II, the consequence has been the gradual establishment of a 'culture of death' in Western liberal societies. There is now an impressive body of literature devoted to the analysis of this phenomenon.[59] In essence, '[f]reedom attains its full development only by accepting the truth. In a world without truth, freedom loses its foundation and man is exposed to the violence of passion and to manipulation, both open and hidden.'[60]

---

55 Zieba, M. 1994, 'Truth and freedom in the thought of Pope John Paul', in J. Wilkins (ed.), Understanding *Veritatis* Splendor, SPCK, London, p. 37.
56 Cahill, L. S. 1993, 'Veritatis splendor', *Commonweal*, vol. CXX (22 October 1993), p. 15.
57 Weigel, *The Cube and the Cathedral*, p. 78.
58 Tilley, R. 2007, *Benedict XVI and the Search for Truth*, St Paul's Publications, Sydney, p. 59.
59 Brennan, W. 2008, *Confronting the Language Empowering the Culture of Death*, Sapientia Press, Florida; Holloway, C. 2008, *John Paul II and the Challenge of Liberal Modernity*, Baylor University Press, Texas; Jeffreys, D. 2004, *Defending Human Dignity: John Paul II and political realism*, Brazos Press, Michigan.
60 John Paul II, *Centesimus Annus*, para. 46.

When the world's religious traditions attempt to speak out about an important issue facing society, they are perceived as attempting to impose their moral preferences on that community. Such behaviour is characterised as an attempt to 'subvert the institutions which are basic to our constitutional system of representative government'.[61]

While it seems to be accepted that democracies are founded on 'a tendency to claim that agnosticism and sceptical relativism are the philosophy and the basic attitude which correspond to democratic forms of political life',[62] the world's religious traditions claim, however, that *genuine democracy* is more than the freedom to implement policies agreed on simply by consensus.

Speaking prophetically, the world's religious traditions argue that democracy is truly free when the freedom to choose between policies is grounded in transcendental moral truths underpinning those policies. A democracy based solely on weight of numbers is fragile because it is divorced from the truth of transcendental moral principles necessary for the 'merits of the arguments in its favour'.[63]

What's wrong with this? A lethal philosophy?

There are two flaws in the critics' conception of democracy. First, the nature of the *kind* of consensus underpinning democracy is misconceived. Second, the elimination of truth from the freedom of consensus underpinning democracy is self-defeating and lethal.

Critics argue that the Church does not reflect the 'consensus' necessary for a 'true' democracy. Jesuit John Courtney Murray argues, however, that consensus in democracy means more than simply majority views.

Murray argues that 'according to the classical tradition of political thought, consensus is a very different thing: it is a doctrine that commands public agreement because of the merits of the arguments in its favour'.[64] This view of public consensus 'transcends sheer experience and expediency; it is basically a moral conception…The reason of the wise is a responsible reason, concerned with fidelity to moral principle…Democracy is more than a political experiment.'[65]

---

61 McGuinness, 'Democracy and the right to die'.
62 John Paul II, *Centesimus Annus*, para. 46.
63 Murray, J. C. 1960, *We Hold These Truths,* Sheed and Ward, United States, p. 36.
64 Ibid., n. 31, p. 139. Dulles cites Murray, *We Hold These Truths,* p. 36.
65 Ibid., n. 31, p. 140.

Therefore a 'democracy' in which the validity of arguments for or against an issue is based solely on weight of numbers is fragile. It is fragile because it separates freedom to choose social policies from transcendental moral truths necessary for the 'merits of the arguments in [the policy's] favour'. This fragility exposes its second and lethal flaw.

The Church asserts a democracy built without reference to transcendental moral truths is lethal. *Centesimus Annus* concludes: 'But...if there is no ultimate truth to guide and direct political activity, then ideas and convictions can easily be manipulated for reasons of power. As history demonstrates, a democracy without values easily turns into open or thinly disguised totalitarianism.'[66]

Why does this happen? According to John Carroll,[67] the Greek word for 'truth', '*aletheia*', contains an inbuilt narrative. Truth is that which is *a-lethe*, and not *lethe*. This refers to Plato's 'Vision of Er', where souls who are destined for reincarnation drink from Lethe's stream inducing forgetfulness before they return to Earth: 'They were all required to drink the water and each one as he drank forgot all things.'[68]

Lethe, being the place of forgetfulness, is an allegory of forgetfulness of transcendental truths constituting our humanity. To drink is to extinguish memory. Oblivion is a state in which individuals have forgotten the truth of who they are. This narrative exists in our language. To be without truth is *lethal*; death in life, its condition that of *lethargy*, is a weariness of spirit. Weigel summarises:

> [H]uman beings could certainly try to organise their lives and affairs entirely on their own. What atheistic humanism had proven was that, without God, human beings could organise the world only in a brutal contest of wills, one against the other. In the suffocating climate of a world without windows or doors, human beings inevitably turn on one another.[69]

Compellingly, research into the abuses by US soldiers at the Abu Ghraib prison in Iraq confirms de Lubac's views. Reicher and Haslam concluded that a 'failure of leaders to champion clear humane and democratic values' created a power vacuum filled by majority view, which resulted in tyranny.[70]

---

66   Ibid., para. 46.
67   Carroll, J. 2001, *The Western Dreaming*, HarperCollins, Australia.
68   Plato, 'The vision of Er', *Republic*, 10.618a, <http://hsa.brown.edu/~maicar/Underworld.html>
69   Weigel, *The Truth of Catholicism*, p. 23.
70   Reicher, S. and Haslam, A. 2004, 'Why not everyone is a torturer', *BBC News*, 22 May 2004, <http://newsvote.bbc.co.uk/mpapps/pagetools/print/news.bbc.co.uk>

Contemporary societies?

In what sense can it be said that Western liberal democracies are vulnerable to dehumanising ideological forces? At first glance, there hardly seems to be a correlation between Nazi Germany, Stalinist Russia, Communist China and our consumer-oriented Western culture. What possible relevance does the above discussion have to twenty-first-century Western democratic life?

I want to suggest that there is a spectrum of possibilities in the existence of totalitarian and dehumanising regimes, with Nazi Germany, Stalinist Russia and Communist China existing at only the extreme end of this spectrum. Is it possible for a society to exist under such a regime without its inhabitants thinking about it in those terms?

The invisible tyranny?

Surely we would *know* if our society began to assume totalitarian or dehumanising proportions. Is it possible that the citizens of such a 'democracy' think they are free when in fact they are anything but free? The gradual erosion of rights and freedoms leaves citizens with the 'freedom' to enjoy only those rights permitted by the State. This was the warning given by Aldous Huxley in his novel *Brave New World*, in which 'His Fordship' Mustafa Mond stated: 'People [here] are happy; they get what they want and they never want what they can't get.'[71]

The citizens of Nazi Germany, Stalinist Russia and Communist China were 'free' to engage in social activities deemed appropriate by the State. Citizens were 'free' to attend book-burning rallies, public denunciations, patriotic rallies and 'state-sponsored' events. They were not permitted, however, to attend meetings critical of the State or engage in freedom of movement across state borders or engage in activities described in nebulous terms as 'subversive' to the State's interest.

Is it possible that Mill's statement that the 'only freedom which deserves the name is that of preserving our own good in our own way, so long as we do not attempt to deprive others of theirs' can coexist with Huxley's observation? In other words: 'What about a nation whose inhabitants are allowed the freedom to do everything they may wish to do as long as they do not violate anyone else's personal freedom, but do not realise that they have been programmed to desire only what their government wants them to desire?'[72]

---

71   Huxley, A. 1966, *Brave New World*, Bantam Books, New York, p. 149.
72   Dennehy, R. 2007, 'The illusion of freedom separated from moral virtue', *Journal of Interdisciplinary Studies*, p. 22.

Surely before this level of tyranny was reached we would see troops in the streets and civil liberties suspended?

Not necessarily. In his text *The Republic*, Plato examined the forces that would bring about the devolution of democracies into tyrannies. Plato suggested that citizens did not suddenly swap their democracy for tyranny. Instead, citizens of democracies surrender their rights and freedoms by slow degrees as they also lose their moral virtue.[73]

At work here is a 'slippery slope' of acquiescence; people compromise their values in small ways at first, which makes it easier for them to make larger compromises later. A recent film titled *Good* provides an excellent illustration.

Actor Viggo Mortensen plays a literature professor at the start of Adolf Hitler's rise to power in Germany in the 1930s. Mortensen's character once wrote a book describing how a terminally ill woman was euthanised by her husband as an act of kindness. The emerging National Socialist Regime invites the professor to write a paper providing justifiable reasons for introducing euthanasia. At first, the professor is reluctant to do so, perhaps sensing the evil ends to which such a paper will be put.

The professor does, however, write the paper and it is indeed used as part of the Nazi's 'social planning' policies. As the Nazi regime solidifies its grip on power, the professor slowly becomes a more important intellectual tool for the regime and progresses in rank, becoming a member of the SS.

The professor makes an increasing number of compromises to his values before realising that his decisions are having deadly consequences. One of those decisions is his failure to help his Jewish best friend, a dentist, escape to France.

The film ends when the professor, in full black SS uniform, traces his Jewish friend to a concentration camp, only to discover that his worst suspicions about the Nazi regime have been confirmed. The professor can only wonder at how he has come to be so far removed from his former position and values since the Nazi rise to power.

What tyranny?

If it is possible for citizens of a Western democratic society to be under a tyrannous influence and yet be unaware of that fact then what might that tyranny look like?

---

73   Plato 1997, *The Republic*, Wordsworth Classics, United Kingdom, pp. 557a–66e.

Among the many popular souvenirs for sale in the Tibetan community in exile in Dharamsala, India, are small cloth wall hangings that contain sayings attributed to His Holiness the Dalai Lama. One of those hangings is titled 'The Paradox of Our Age' and purports to be a critical reflection on contemporary liberal democratic societies. It reads:

> We have bigger houses but smaller families; more conveniences but less time. We have more degrees but less sense; more knowledge but less judgement; more experts but more problems; more medicines, but less healthiness. We have been all the way to the moon and back, but have trouble crossing the street to meet the new neighbour. We build more computers to hold more information to produce more copies than ever, but have less communication. We have become long on quantity but short on quality. These are times of fast foods but slow digestion; tall man but short character; steep profits but shallow relationships. It is a time when there is much in the window but nothing in the room.

It turns out that there *is* something amiss with contemporary Western societies. Despite increasing levels of wealth and prosperity, we are unhappier than ever before. We are supposedly the beneficiaries of the scientific and industrial revolutions and yet seem to have a chronic shortage of time to spend cultivating relationships and a happy quality of life:

> Nineteenth century economists predicted that the abundance made possible by technological advance and the modern organisation of work would result in the emergence of 'post-materialist' humans—people existing on a higher plane, where their cultural, intellectual and spiritual powers are refined…Futurists saw a society transformed by the fruits of sustained growth—a society in which humankind, freed of the chore of making a living, would devote itself to activities that are truly fulfilling.[74]

So what happened?

The ideological assumptions discussed above have become part of the fabric of our thinking of what it means to be part of a Western liberal democracy. Those assumptions include the belief that there is no real, objective truth that can make a claim on the freedom we enjoy since we can behave as we choose provided we do not 'hurt' anyone else. But what does 'hurt' mean when another of the prevalent ideological assumptions seems to be the denigration of the value of others, except in so far as they become means to satisfying my own ends—a perversion of Immanuel Kant's warning that others are ends in themselves?

---

74 Hamilton, C. 2005, *Affluenza*, Allen & Unwin, Sydney, p. 5.

The denial of transcendental truths about what it means to be human leads to a very pragmatic view of people and things. And in Western societies that pragmatism is directed overwhelmingly towards consumption. The value of people and objects is defined by reference to what they can do for us, what benefit we can derive from them. When the values of 'being' are replaced with the values of 'having', a very modern tyranny takes hold with

> [a]n ideology informed by the principles of economic efficiency, inordinate consumerism, physical beauty and pleasure. It is a *practical materialism* which breeds individualism, utilitarianism and hedonism. It threatens human dignity because it searches for what it can do, rather than what it *ought* to do.[75]

Could this malaise ever *really* infect our comfortable lifestyles? According to much research, it already has. In fact, an entirely new term, 'affluenza', has been created to describe the condition in which we are confused about what it takes to live a meaningful life.[76]

'Affluenza' has been described as

> [t]he collective addiction, character flaws, psychological wounds, neuroses and behavioural disorders caused or exacerbated by the presence of, or desire for money/wealth…In individuals, it takes the form of a dysfunctional or unhealthy relationship with money, regardless of one's socio-economic level. It manifests as behaviours resulting from a preoccupation with—or imbalance around—the money in our lives.[77]

The world's spiritual traditions warn against measuring our own self-worth and the worth of others by reference to 'having'. Rather, they remind us prophetically that the value of others exists simply because of their 'being'. Whether described as 'made in the image and likeness of God' or as possessing the 'fundamental potential for enlightenment', all spiritual traditions call us back to the most basic truth that others are to be valued as ends in themselves, possessing a fundamental dignity that does not depend on economic status, money in the bank or the level of economic contribution to society.

The proliferation of retreat houses, weekend escapes, the need for 'quiet time' and the growing feeling that 'something is missing' are all indications that economic policies promoting higher consumption and the better allocation of resources have failed to produce an increase in our happiness.

---

75 Tilley, *Benedict XVI and the Search for Truth*, p. 66.
76 Hamilton, *Affluenza*, p. 7.
77 Ibid.

The world's spiritual traditions remind us that there is another way of being human, another way of finding the inner and other freedom to love that is not dependent on consumption patterns. While the world's religious traditions would not ever advocate repealing the benefits of the Enlightenment and the scientific and democratic revolutions, they do call attention to the dangers inherent in divorcing being from doing.

Religions are not to blame; but like all other ideological forces, they can be alloyed to baser forces such as nationalism, ethnocentrism and consumerism. True religious values are ennobling, inspiring and challenging, reminding us that we are valuable simply because we exist and that the way to true human fulfilment is to love—genuinely, freely and unconditionally.

8. Introduction to Christianity
PROFESSOR RAYMOND CANNING,
AUSTRALIAN CATHOLIC UNIVERSITY

The number of Christians worldwide in 2000 has been numbered at 1.9 billion—that is, 33 per cent of the world's population. On current predictions, by 2025, the number will grow to 2.6 billion. By 2050, however, the proportion of the world's population that is Christian will remain, as it was in 1900, at just more than one-third. The difference is that the majority will not be European or white—in fact, the overall proportion of non-Latino whites might be no more than one in five. The prevailing shift of numbers from Europe to Africa, Latin America and Asia (where numbers increased from 94 million to one billion during the century from 1900 to 2000) will have continued. Furthermore, it is estimated that membership of Pentecostal churches will have grown to one billion—proportionally much larger than it had earlier been.

This chapter will provide background to the development of the Christian churches as together constituting the world's largest faith. The major source for this brief sketch will be the Christian scriptures and early church traditions. The approach will be predominantly theological rather than historical or sociological. It is recognised that, while many diverse forms of Christian belief and practice preceded the acceptance from the second to the fourth centuries of the authoritative body of Christian literature known as the 'canon', a decision was clearly made with the establishment of this scriptural canon for a unified form of Christianity that would become progressively stronger. The criteria by which works were admitted to the canon were: 1) the proclamation of the one God as Creator of the whole world, spiritual and material; 2) the affirmation of the reality of the life, death and resurrection of Jesus Christ; and 3) the acceptance of the scriptures of the Jewish people, which, when incorporated into the Christian Bible, generally came to be known as the Old Testament.

To be sure, major divisions within Christianity would again follow in the succeeding centuries. Foremost among them were, first, the formal separation of the Eastern and Western churches, based in respectively Constantinople and Rome, in 1054, with the subsequent growth of Eastern Orthodoxy; and second, the splitting of Protestant and Catholic churches in the wake of the Reformation of the sixteenth century. This latter division continued to mark Western Christianity in the course of its missionary expansion in the next four centuries. A confessional and denominational divide therefore accompanied the growth of Christian churches throughout the world—and churches tended to reproduce and split over and over again. The modern ecumenical movement—which began to take shape at the end of the nineteenth century and especially at the beginning of the twentieth century—is still wrestling with these manifold divisions in its efforts to work towards Christian unity.

On the other hand, alongside denominational differences, many different forms of Christianity have arisen, at least for a time, as Christian faith has permeated different cultures and has in turn been influenced by these cultures and the religions that it has met in them. The question arises, then, about what it is that gives coherence to the use of the name 'Christian' and how it is that Christians of very different kinds are still able to recognise and communicate with one another as Christians.

Although there exist among Christians themselves distinct, and even radical, differences of approach to the scriptures of the Old and New Testaments, these scriptures constitute a touchstone that the many diverse Christian churches and forms of Christianity have in common. We begin our engagement with them by asking what they have to say about the life, ministry, death and resurrection of Jesus of Nazareth, who would come to be confessed by his disciples as the Christ (the Messiah).

In a second part, we will provide an exemplary model of Christian life and community from the First Letter of John written towards the end of the first century CE. Here, the reality of the incarnation of the Word is central and the recognition that 'God is love' is spelt out theologically and ethically. The sermons on this letter by the renowned Augustine, Bishop of Hippo, in North Africa at the beginning of the fifth century give further insight into these essential dimensions of Christian faith.

Third, we will briefly consider the Christian creed, the so-called Nicene–Constantinopolitan Creed, which was recognised in 381 as expressing the Church's core beliefs, and which was adopted formally by the Church in Council in 451. Finally, we will point to a very specific and challenging contemporary phenomenon—the Christian churches' openness to dialogue with religions other than Christianity. This will be illustrated principally by reference to the post-Vatican Council II Catholic Church.

Jesus of Nazareth: life, ministry, death and resurrection

Any account of the origins of the Christian movement has to begin with Jesus of Nazareth.

With a fair degree of probability and reliability, the following brief historical and theological account of Jesus can be given.[1] He was born about 4 BCE and was brought up in Galilee. His family line linked him to the great Jewish King David. At his baptism by John the Baptist in the River Jordan, he experienced his call while beholding a vision of the Spirit descending on him like a dove: 'And a voice came from heaven, "You are my Son, the Beloved; with you I am well pleased."'[2]

Proclamation of the Kingdom of God: parables, miracles, meals, Sermon on the Mount

Central to his call was the proclamation of the kingdom of God, which he presented in parables highlighting the good news ('gospel') of God's superabundant mercy and compassion. The gospel writer Matthew records one of Jesus's short parables in these terms: 'Again, the kingdom of heaven is like a merchant in search of fine pearls; on finding one pearl of great value, he went and sold all that he had and bought it.'[3] Luke, another gospel writer, represents the shape of the kingdom in Jesus's well-known parable of the Good Samaritan. As told by Jesus, this story confounds all his hearers' expectations, for it identifies the conduct of the neighbour par excellence not with the deeds of one's own countrymen and co-religionists, but with those of the hated Samaritan, the outsider, who alone effectively shows mercy to the man left half-dead by the roadside.[4]

Signs of the kingdom of God are also present in Jesus's healing miracles and exorcisms. When accused of using the devil's power to drive out demons, Jesus responds with a striking alternative: 'But if it is by the finger of God that I cast out the demons, then the kingdom of God has come to you.'[5] Similarly, his practice of sharing meals with both the clean and the unclean (tax collectors, sinners, the afflicted, the marginalised and so on) testifies to his acceptance of, and readiness to offer forgiveness and healing to, those who would otherwise have been considered excluded from God's embrace and disbarred from welcome in the community.

Jesus's Sermon on the Mount—exemplified in the command to love one's enemies,[6] as well as in *The Lord's Prayer*, for which forgiveness is central,[7] and

---

[1] For the trend of the following account, see Ford, D. 1999, *Theology: A very short introduction*, Oxford University Press, Oxford, pp. 93–7.
[2] Mark 1:11. All scriptural quotations are from *The Holy Bible: New revised standard version*, 1998, HarperCollins, London.
[3] Matthew 13:45–56.
[4] Luke 10:25–37.
[5] Luke 11:20.
[6] Matthew 5:44.
[7] Matthew 6:9–15.

the golden rule to 'do to others as you would have them do to you'[8]—embodies Jesus's vision that the kingdom of God is already breaking in, and points in a particular way to a reversal of the status quo: a God-centred renewal of people in all the dimensions of their lives and a transformation of the world. All of this, Jesus understands, is being brought about in his own person. At the very heart of the Sermon on the Mount are the Beatitudes, which, in their earliest form, might have read as follows:

> Happy are the poor,
> for theirs is the kingdom of heaven.
> Happy are the mourners,
> for they shall be comforted.
> Happy are the hungry,
> for they shall be satisfied.[9]

Thus, in Jesus's proclamation of the kingdom of God, the world was being turned upside down, and his message of tremendous love and forgiveness came to be identified more and more with his own person as messenger.

Death by crucifixion

Jesus's sense of freedom, his compassion and his inclusive aims gave rise to conflict and hostility. He met this hostility head on when, like a messianic king bringing peace, he rode into Jerusalem on a donkey at the time of the great Jewish festival Passover, when the city would have been full of pilgrims and tensions with the Roman authorities would have been at their highest. Matters went from bad to worse, however, when he drove the traders and moneychangers from the temple, symbolising that the temple itself—the centre of Jewish religious and cultural life—would be destroyed. The Jewish and Roman leaders joined together, then, to have him arrested and charged, leading to his crucifixion by the Romans for stirring up revolt. With his degrading death on the cross at Calvary, Jesus paid the price for the kind of life he had lived by loving others without reserve. Dying on the cross, he was reduced even to crying out in abandonment, 'My God, my God, why have you forsaken me?'[10]

Jesus's death as a source of life

For all this, however, death did not have the last word in relation to Jesus. Not only did his disciples in trying to make sense of the seeming failure of his

---

8   Matthew 7:12.
9   See Rausch, T. P. 2003, *Who is Jesus? An introduction to Christology*, Liturgical Press, Collegeville, Minnesota, pp. 80–1.
10 Mark 15:34.

mission eventually come to understand him as the rejected prophet and the suffering, just one, they recognised him as the servant who came 'to give his life as a ransom for many'.[11] This is the same meaning that Jesus himself applied to his approaching death when he shared a meal with his disciples at Passover—a meal that has come to be known as the Last (or the Lord's) Supper. The Jewish people at Passover celebrated their liberation by God from Egypt. Lambs were slaughtered and eaten to symbolise this great event. Similarly, in this very same context in which Israel's redemption was being commemorated, Jesus on the night before his death, in a meal of bread and wine, identified himself as the true Passover lamb who would be slaughtered on the cross the next day—known by us as Good Friday. The words spoken by John the Baptist on seeing Jesus at the beginning of the Gospel of John therefore came to resonate with their full force: 'Here is the Lamb of God who takes away the sin of the world!'[12]

In this alignment with the Jewish feast of Passover, the saving significance of Jesus's death is clearly brought out. This theme of Jesus as Saviour will become central to Christian reflection. As we read, for example, in 1 John 2:2, '[h]e is the atoning sacrifice for our sins, and not only for ours but also for the sins of the whole world', while for Paul, Christ 'died for all, so that those who live might live no longer for themselves, but for him who died and was raised for them'.[13]

Jesus's resurrection: foundational Christian experience

The Christian Church's proclamation of Jesus as Saviour of the world would be inconceivable apart from the faith of his disciples that, contrary to all expectations, he had been raised from the dead. Likewise, the very existence of those scriptures that now constitute the New Testament would be unthinkable were it not for Jesus's followers' conviction that God's love for him had proved stronger than death and their sure experience that he was still present with them, although now in a way very different from before. To the women who had come to the tomb on the third day after Jesus's death, the gospel writer Matthew presented an angel from heaven as saying:

> Do not be afraid; I know that you are looking for Jesus who was crucified. He is not here, for he has been raised, as he said. Come, see the place where he lay. Then go quickly and tell his disciples, 'He has been raised from the dead' and indeed he is going ahead of you to Galilee; there you will see him.[14]

---

11 Matthew 20:28.
12 John 1:29.
13 2 Corinthians 5:15.
14 Matthew 28:5–7.

And see him the disciples did. Two of them on the road to Emmaus conversed with him at length after he joined them on the road and they showed him hospitality. But it was only when they came to share bread with him—in a scene that is evocative of his last supper with his disciples only a few evenings before—that 'their eyes were opened and they recognized him'. Even though 'he vanished from their sight' at that very point,[15] they had indeed recognised him and so realised why their hearts had been burning within them while he was talking to them on the road and explaining how the scriptures of the people of Israel referred to the Messiah who was to come. On returning to Jerusalem, they found that the word was out, for Jesus's followers there were saying: 'The Lord has risen indeed, and he has appeared to Simon.'[16]

As well as the stories of Jesus's post-resurrection appearances to the disciples—which Paul catalogues as happening to Cephas (Peter), the 12, more than 500 brothers and sisters (most of whom are still alive), James, all the apostles, and lastly to himself 'as one untimely born'[17]—there is the tradition, witnessed in all four of the gospels (Matthew, Mark, Luke and John), of the empty tomb. When the women visited the tomb on the third day after Jesus's death and burial, they found to their great surprise that Jesus's body was not there.

It is noteworthy that the historical credibility of these accounts is heightened by the fact that all of the witnesses presented are women. If, in that highly patriarchal culture, the story had been invented, the authors would hardly have based their case on women's testimony, which was considered quite worthless.[18]

Be this as it may, it is undeniably true that all of those who give witness to Jesus's appearances and to the empty tomb are people committed in faith to the risen Christ. However one might weigh up the historical truth of these stories, as historical events, they are inseparably bound up with the testimony of believers to their own experience of enjoying a continuing relationship with Jesus as having been raised by the Father from the dead. These people, whose lives have been transformed by the Spirit that comes from the risen Jesus,[19] are found striving to make sense of an utterly unexpected, unprecedented event—namely, that the Lord has indeed risen.

In reporting what had been handed down to him by his predecessors in Christian faith, Paul recorded 'that Christ died for our sins in accordance with the scriptures, and that he was buried [for he had really died], and that he was raised on the third day in accordance with the scriptures'.[20] Note that

---

15 Luke 24:31.
16 Luke 24:34.
17 1 Corinthians 15:5–8.
18 See McGrath, A. E. 1997, *An Introduction to Christianity*, Blackwell, Oxford, pp. 103.
19 Acts 2:32–3.
20 1 Corinthians 15:3–4.

Jesus's resurrection before the end of time was a totally unpredictable outcome. Reflecting further on the testimony that he has inherited, Paul expresses his own conviction that 'if Christ has not been raised, then our proclamation has been in vain and your faith has been in vain',[21] thus giving voice to the core insight of believers before and since that the resurrection of Jesus is central to the faith of the Christian Church.

Resurrection, Pentecost, baptism and human culture

Christians expressed their faith not only in the risen Christ; through the gift of the Holy Spirit at Pentecost, they found themselves transformed by being united with Christ in his resurrection. Through their baptism, Christians came to share in the risen life of Christ. As Paul says:

> Therefore we have been buried with [Christ] by baptism into death, so that, just as Christ was raised from the dead by the glory of the Father, so too we might walk in newness of life. For if we have been united with him in a death like his, we will certainly be united with him in a resurrection like his.[22]

And again:

> I want to know Christ and the power of his resurrection and the sharing of his sufferings by becoming like him in his death, if somehow I may attain the resurrection from the dead.[23]

Adherents of other religious traditions too sense how central Jesus's resurrection is to Christian faith and life, and by implication, to life in all its dimensions. As the Japanese Zen Master Joshu Sasaki Roshi is quoted as saying, 'I like Christianity. But I would not like Christianity without the resurrection. Show me your resurrection. I want to see your resurrection.'

The Easter faith of Christians has also generated a majestic sweep of artistic and cultural achievements, from the chants of the Russian Orthodox Easter Liturgy to Titian's *Noli me tangere*—the sixteenth-century painting of the post-resurrection meeting of Mary Magdalene and Jesus in the garden, which has been described as highlighting 'the moment in everyone's life when it becomes clear that love is transformed, but not diminished, by the destruction of the body'.[24]

---

21 1 Corinthians 15:14.
22 Romans 6:4–5.
23 Philippians 3:10–11.
24 MacGregor, N. and Langmuir, E. 2000, *Seeing Salvation: Images of Christ in art*, BBC, London, p. 191.

The philosopher Ludwig Wittgenstein, by no stretch of the imagination a conventional Christian, asks: 'What inclines even me to believe in Christ's Resurrection?' He reflects as follows:

> If he did not rise from the dead, then he decomposed in the grave like another man...but if I am to be REALLY saved—what I need is certainty—not wisdom, dreams or speculation—and this certainty is faith. And faith is faith in what is needed by my *heart*, my *soul*, not my speculative intelligence...Perhaps we can say: only *love* can believe in the Resurrection. Or: it is *love* that believes the Resurrection.[25]

One senses that Mary Magdalene in Titian's *Noli me tangere* would have known very well what Wittgenstein meant when he wrote that 'it is *love* that believes the Resurrection'.

The risen Jesus worshipped as God

On the basis of their foundational experience of the risen Jesus, the early believers soon came to direct their devotion and worship to him in hymns, prayers and invocations and in the celebrations of baptism and the Eucharist (the Lord's Supper). This meant that Jesus came to be worshipped along with God in a manner that had been reserved for God alone in the Jewish monotheistic tradition. Out of the experience of praying to Jesus, these believers came to confess not only that 'the Word was with God', but that 'the Word was God'.[26] In the Christian scriptures, the highest point in this realisation of the full divine identity of Jesus is found on the lips of the so-called doubting Thomas when, responding to the risen one who has appeared to the fearful disciples, he addresses Jesus as 'My Lord and my God!'.[27]

Thomas's Lord and God, however, is not a ghost or a mirage. He is, rather, the one who invites Thomas to put his finger into the marks of the nails in his hands and his hand into his wounded side.[28] To be sure, this is not exactly the same bodily Jesus who had been with his disciples before his death, for 'although the doors were shut, [this] Jesus came and stood among them'.[29] Nonetheless, there is no split between the heavenly, spiritual, divine (now risen) being of Jesus and his fleshly, earthly, historical person.

---

25 As cited by Kelly, A. J. 2007, *The Resurrection Effect: Transforming Christian life and thought*, Orbis Books, Maryknoll, NY, p. 22.
26 John 1:1.
27 John 20:28.
28 John 20:24–9.
29 John 20:26.

There is no pretence about his human, bodily presence, either during his life on Earth or in his risen state. Contrary to the position that would later be strongly asserted by the Gnostics, especially in the second century, he was not a divine spiritual being merely present in human disguise. No, God's Word had truly taken flesh in Jesus, and that flesh was integral to his identity—not to be discarded. Similarly, as the Church would later labour to make plain, Jesus's true humanity was not diminished or compromised by his being confessed as 'true God from true God'.

The Word of life and God as love

From the perspective of Christian believers therefore Jesus is understood as the founder of Christianity not in the sense that it was Christianity that the historical Jesus preached, but rather on account of the fact that he was accepted by believers in faith as the incarnate Son of God, and as the revelation of God made visible in the world: 'And the Word became flesh and lived among us, and we have seen his glory, the glory of the Father's only Son, full of grace and truth.'[30] This incarnate Christ is believed to be 'the image of the invisible God…For in him all the fullness of God was pleased to dwell'.[31] It is therefore precisely the faith of Christians in the incarnation of the Word that turns the Jesus who can be known historically into the very foundation of Christianity. This foundation, Christians believe, lies in the very self-revelation of God.

The incarnation (becoming flesh) of the Word is the direct subject of the First Letter of John. The reason this letter was written was to counter the fragmentation and breakdown of an early Christian community caused by those who rejected the community's faith that Jesus, who had always existed as Son with the Father, had been sent by the Father into the world. Its opening words speak of the proclamation of 'what was from the beginning, what we have heard, what we have seen with our eyes, what we have looked at and touched with our hands, concerning the word of life'.[32]

As this word of life is identified with 'the eternal life that was with the Father and was revealed to us',[33] Jesus is thus presented as both eternally with the Father and, at one and the same time, a sensible, visible, touchable presence in the midst of the community. As the early fifth-century church father Augustine commented:

---

30   John 1:14.
31   Colossians 1:15, 19.
32   John 1:1.
33   John 1:2.

> We were able to see flesh [with our eyes], but we were unable to see the Word [which can be seen by the heart alone]. [Therefore], the Word was made flesh, which we would be able to see, so that what was in us—whereby we might see the Word [that is, the heart]—would be healed.[34]

The Father takes the initiative by manifesting the Word of life in the flesh. For Augustine, this leads to a healing of hearts whereby the Word of life itself is seen. Elsewhere Augustine refers to this healing of hearts as salvation, showing how it comes about through God's love revealed in the humility of Christ for our sakes. As he says in one place: 'If this was all that God the Word did, to become flesh, it would be unbelievable humility.'[35]

While the First Letter of John does not speak immediately in terms of healing or salvation, what it does bring to the fore is communion with one another and with God. 'We declare to you what we have seen and heard so that you also may have fellowship with us; and truly our fellowship is with the Father and with his Son Jesus Christ.'[36] The love that is at the heart of this fellowship or communion is expressed throughout the letter, but nowhere more forcefully than in the following passage:

> Beloved, let us love one another, because love is from God; everyone who loves is born of God and knows God. Whoever does not love does not know God, for God is love. God's love was revealed among us in this way: God sent his only Son into the world so that we might live through him. In this is love, not that we loved God but that he loved us and sent his Son to be the atoning sacrifice for our sins. Beloved, since God loved us so much, we also ought to love one another. No one has ever seen God; if we love one another, God lives in us, and his love is perfected in us…God is love. Whoever lives in love lives in God, and God in him.[37]

In his commentary on this passage, Augustine notes that not only is love said to be 'from God', but 'God is love'. He also, however, daringly inverts the words so as to read not only that 'God is love', but that 'love is God'.

This leads Augustine to a reflection on the love that is both 'from God' and 'God'—namely, the Holy Spirit. In relation to the statement of 1 John 4:12 that 'if we love one another, God will abide in us, and his love will be perfected in

---

34 English translation from Ramsey, B. (trans.) 2008, *Homilies on the First Letter of John, in the Works of Saint Augustine: A translation for the 21st century. Part III—Homilies. Volume 14*, D. E. Doyle OSA and T. M. OSA (eds), New City Press, Hyde Park, NY, 1.1. Explanatory insertions in the quotation above are the present author's own.
35 '*Sermon* Mai' in ibid., 16.3.
36 John 1:3.
37 1 John 4:7–13, 16.

us', Augustine explains that if your heart 'is filled with love, you have God's Spirit…"Because the love of God has been poured out in our hearts through the Holy Spirit, who has been given to us" (Romans 5:5)'.[38]

Later, in his work on the Triune God, Augustine will return to this identification of love with God. We read there that 'this same fraternal love itself (for it is fraternal love by which we love one another) is proclaimed by so great an authority as the Apostle John [in 1 John 4:7–8] not only to come "from God" but also to be God'.[39]

And, at the end of that same great work on *The Trinity*, he will again clarify that '[t]herefore, the love which is from God and which is God is properly the Holy Spirit, through whom the love of God is poured out in our hearts. Through this love the whole Trinity [Father, Son and Holy Spirit] dwells in us.'[40] The movement is from love for one another to the Holy Spirit, whose gift this love is, to the indwelling of the Triune God in the Christian community.

When Christians love one another, therefore, God lives in them and they live in God. Love for one another is the leitmotiv of the First Letter of John, and this love for one's neighbour is integral to the process by which God's love 'is truly made complete'.[41] The contours and directions of the Christian moral life are firmly sketched in this letter, as the following texts from John make clear:

> Whoever says 'I am in the light', while hating a brother or sister is still in the darkness. Whoever loves a brother or sister lives in the light, and in such a person there is no cause for stumbling. (2:9–10)

> Do not love the world or the things in the world. The love of the Father is not in those who love the world. (2:15)

> See what love the Father has given us, that we should be called children of God; and that is what we are. (3:1)

> For this is the message you have heard from the beginning, that we should love one another…We know that we have passed from death to life because we love one another. Whoever does not love abides in death…We know love by this, that he laid down his life for us—and we ought to lay down our lives for one another. How does God's love

---

38   Ramsey, *Homilies on the First Letter of John,* 8.12. Translation amended by author.
39   Saint Augustine 399/400–416/421, *The* Trinity, VIII.8.12. Translations *from The* Trinity are the author's own.
40   Ibid., XV.18.32.
41   1 John 2:5.

abide in anyone who has the world's goods and sees a brother or sister in need and yet refuses to help? Little children, let us love not in word or speech, but in truth and action. (3:11, 14, 16–18)

This is [God's] command, that we should believe in the name of his Son Jesus Christ and love one another just as he has commanded us. (3:23)

We love because he first loved us. Those who say, 'I love God', and hate their brothers or sisters are liars; for those who do not love a brother or sister whom they have seen, cannot love God whom they have not seen. The commandment we have from him is this: those who love God must love their brothers and sisters also. (4:19–21)

By this we know that we love the children of God, when we love God and obey his commandments. For the love of God is this, that we obey his commandments. (5:2–3)

Augustine in his commentary draws the links with a whole range of other New Testament passages on the theme of love. For example:

I give you a new commandment, that you love one another. Just as I have loved you, you also should love one another.[42]

But I say to you, 'Love your enemies and pray for those who persecute you.'[43]

Bear one another's burdens, and in this way you will fulfil the law of Christ.[44]

[Bear] with one another in love, making every effort to maintain the unity of the Spirit in the bond of peace.[45]

Above all, maintain constant love for one another, for love covers a multitude of sins.[46]

And if I have prophetic powers, and understand all mysteries and all knowledge, and if I have all faith, so as to remove mountains, but do not have love, I am nothing. If I give away all my possessions, and if I hand over my body to be burned, but do not have love, I gain nothing.[47]

---

42   John 13:34.
43   Matthew 5:44.
44   Galatians 6:2.
45   Ephesians 4:2–3.
46   1 Peter 4:8.
47   1 Corinthians 13:2–3.

> No one has greater love than this, to lay down one's life for one's friends.[48]

> [L]ove is the fulfilling of the law.[49]

> But the end of the commandment is love that comes from a pure heart, a good conscience and sincere faith.[50]

> 'You shall love the Lord your God with all your heart, and with all your soul, and with all your mind.' This is the greatest and first commandment. And a second is like it: 'You shall love your neighbour as yourself.' On these two commandments hang all the law and the prophets.[51]

> If one member [of the body] suffers, all suffer together with it; if one member is honoured, all rejoice together with it. Now you are the body of Christ and individually members of it.[52]

In one of his commentaries on the verses—'for those who do not love a brother or sister whom they have seen, cannot love God whom they have not seen'[53]— Augustine again draws on the daring identification between love and God that has already been observed: 'If God is love, then whoever loves love loves God...A person who loves his brother necessarily loves love itself, and love is God. Therefore whoever loves his brother necessarily loves God.'[54]

In another place, again stressing the unity of love for God and neighbour, he invokes 1 Corinthians 12:26–7 on Christians as members of the Body of Christ. Against this background, he emphasises the unifying power of love, which has been so important to 1 John in the face of disruption and breakdown in that community.

> Do you think that when you love your brother you are loving him alone and not Christ as well? That is impossible, because you are loving the members of Christ. When you love Christ's members you love Christ himself. When you love Christ, you love the Son of God. When you love the Son of God, you love the Father. Love cannot be split up. Begin loving somewhere and the rest will follow…

> Whoever loves God also loves his commandments. And God's commandments are: 'A new commandment I give you: you are to love one another' (Jn 13:34). No one has to excuse himself for passing over

---

48   John 15:13.
49   Romans 13:10.
50   1 Timothy 1:5.
51   Matthew 22:37–40.
52   1 Corinthians 12:26–7.
53   1 John 4:20.
54   Ramsey, *Homilies on the First Letter of John,* 9.10. Author's own translation.

from the one love to the other. This love is so entirely of one piece. Just as love itself has been woven into unity, so it unifies all who come under its influence. Like a fire it smelts them together. When gold is smelted it forms one ingot. But without the fire of love it will never be possible to bring many people together in unity.[55]

For 1 John, then, the unity of a particular Christian community was linked inextricably with 'love not in word or speech, but in truth and action'.[56] Augustine extends this by making the 'love that is so entirely of one piece' the precondition for the unity of the Church as a whole. Moreover, anyone who is without the love that is prepared to give itself for others is seen as effectively denying that 'Christ has come in the flesh'.[57] In this way, faith in the incarnation of the Word goes to the very heart of the moral practice of Christians.

Councils and creeds

Jesus as divine

As we saw above, the doubting Thomas addressed the risen Jesus as '[m]y Lord and my God'. While 'God' is used only rarely in an explicit way of Jesus in the New Testament, the high title 'Lord' is often applied to him in the light of his resurrection from the dead. For example, Paul states that 'if you confess with your lips that Jesus is Lord and believe in your heart that God raised him from the dead, you will be saved'.[58] Thus, the very title 'Lord' that in the scriptures of the people of Israel is reserved for God alone is now also applied to Jesus.

A striking instance of this development is found in 1 Corinthians 8:5–6, where Paul draws a contrast between the many gods and lords of the Graeco-Roman world and the Christian understanding of God: 'Yet for us,' he says, in comparison with what others believe, 'there is one God, the Father…and one Lord, Jesus Christ'. In this manner, by the simple use of the conjunction 'and', Paul effectively ascribes divinity to Jesus as well as to the Father, in such a way that now also clearly distinguishes Christian faith from its origins in Judaism.[59]

---

55 Ibid., 10.3. Author's own translation.
56 3:18.
57 *Ramsey, Homilies on the First Letter of* John, 6.13.
58 Romans 10:9.
59 See Johnson, L. T. 2003, *The Creed: What Christians believe and why it matters,* Darton, Longman & Todd, London, pp. 17–18.

Arius and the Council of Nicaea

Over the ensuing centuries, this question of how Jesus was related to God the Father came to prominence. In the priest Arius's formulation at the beginning of the fourth century, Jesus was seen as a quite exceptional and unique being but, in the end, unequal to the Father. Indeed, he was 'divine' in only a purely honorific sense, having been brought into existence from non-existence and thus belonging to the realm of the creature rather than to that of the Creator. In the view of Arius's opponents, such as the renowned Athanasius, however, if it were the case that Jesus, the Son, was not fully possessed of true divine power, he could not be the saviour of human beings. For Athanasius and what eventually proved to be the majority party, if it were not very God who had come into the world in Christ, human beings would still be mired in their sins.

The Creed of Nicaea of 325, from the first Ecumenical (worldwide) Council, declared Jesus to be of one being and one substance with the Father. In other words, he was confessed as belonging firmly in the realm of the Creator; this was 'true God from true God'—not one who had been brought into existence from non-existence, as if he were a creature, albeit a highly exceptional one. What this confession of faith said about God was that to be God did not mean to be alone and aloof.

What it said about humanity was that, in the Lord Jesus Christ's incarnation, he became a man who was inward to the life of God, thus making possible the divinisation of all human life. The formula of Nicaea, however, was far from universally accepted, and in the debate that raged in the coming decades many different positions were put forward, culminating at one extreme in the view that the Son was quite unlike the Father, and the Holy Spirit even more so.

The Cappadocians and the Nicene–Constantinopolitan Creed of 381

The role of three very learned Greek-speaking theologians was to prove decisive in the years leading up to the second Ecumenical Council, which was held at Constantinople in 381. These were Basil of Caesarea (c. 330–79), Gregory Nazianzen (c. 330–90) and Basil's younger brother, Gregory of Nyssa (c. 335–94), known collectively as the Cappadocians (from the central region of what is modern-day Turkey). Each in his own way insisted, against the Arians and their successors, on the full divinity of the Son, Jesus Christ, while at the same time upholding the Son's eternal distinctness from the Father in his very relationship with Him. Moreover, the Cappadocians argued strenuously that the Holy Spirit also, just as the Son, was fully and equally divine.

The Nicene–Constantinopolitan Creed of 381 (usually known simply as the Nicene Creed, which is the standard creed still prayed at Christian services of worship throughout the world) confesses the Church's faith in 'one God' beginning with the Father as the all-powerful Creator of all that is. It then expresses faith in the one Lord, Jesus Christ, as 'the only Son of God, eternally begotten of the Father'. The addition of the word 'eternally' makes plain the understanding that there was no time when the Son did not exist. Indeed, any insinuation of inequality or subordination is to be rejected, for the Son is confessed as 'true God from true God, begotten, not made [as a creature is "made"], of one being with the Father'. All creation is through the Son. This Son, who lives eternally with the Father, became incarnate as a human being from the Virgin Mary, by the power of the Holy Spirit. He was crucified 'under Pontius Pilate' (a very precise historical reference), suffered, died and was buried. He rose again and ascended into heaven, where he sits at the Father's right hand. The same Lord and Christ will come again in judgment and, to make clear that the Son being a distinct person truly belongs to the inner reality of God and is not simply a time-bound function of Jesus's short life on Earth, it is confessed that 'his kingdom will have no end'.

The following so-called third article of the Nicene Creed clearly defines the divinity of the Holy Spirit for the first time in church teaching.

- 'We believe in the Holy Spirit, the Lord, the giver of life': only God can ultimately give life; therefore, the Holy Spirit is divine.
- 'Who proceeds from the Father (and the Son)': the words in brackets—*Filioque* in Latin—were added later, and have, rightly or wrongly, become symbolic of the theological differences between the Eastern and Western churches, even up to the present day, with the Western church being seen as focusing on the Son while the Eastern church is said to emphasise the Holy Spirit.
- 'With the Father and the Son he is worshipped and glorified': Father, Son and Holy Spirit are to be worshipped equally in their divinity.
- 'He has spoken through the prophets': the Spirit was already at work before the coming of Christ. The Spirit did not come into being only when descending on the disciples at Pentecost and bringing the Church into being, any more than the Son came into being only with Jesus's birth and life on Earth.

On the basis of this understanding of the Father, the Son and the Holy Spirit, the third article of the Nicene Creed then moves forward to express faith in 'one holy catholic and apostolic Church' and 'one baptism for the forgiveness of sins' and to articulate its hope for 'the resurrection of the dead and the life of the world to come'.[60]

Jesus Christ, one person confessed in two natures

If some clarity was reached in the Nicene–Constantinopolitan Creed of 381 regarding the Trinity—Father, Son and Holy Spirit—as the specifically Christian way of naming God, the question of who Jesus himself was, as both God and a human being, continued to exercise the minds of Christians and engender deep disputes. It would be true to say that the creeds of 325 and 381 emphasised the divinity of Jesus, because it was his full and true divinity that was being challenged at that time.

Certain ways of emphasising the divine presence in Jesus, however, could have the effect of diminishing his human being. Did Jesus really have a human soul? The same Council of Constantinople affirmed that he did. The question that came to be debated most hotly in the first half of the fifth century was: was Jesus basically a single reality or was he a double reality? Where should the emphasis be? Should it be on the oneness of Jesus's person as the Word of God or on his two distinct natures, with the divine dwelling in the human? This dispute crystallised with regard to the designation to be given to Mary. Was she to be seen as the God bearer (*Theotokos*) or just as the mother of the human being of Jesus?

The Council of Ephesus of 431 insisted that Mary should be honoured as *Theotokos*, the Mother of God, for to speak otherwise would be to posit a duality of persons in Jesus. The Council of Chalcedon that followed in 451 proved to be a landmark for subsequent Christian understanding of the identity of Jesus. Yes, Jesus is 'of one being with the Father' (as in the Nicene Creed) and, yes also, he is 'of one being with us' human beings. 'One and the same Christ, Son, Lord, only-begotten' is thus 'confessed in two natures' and the distinction between the divine and human natures of this Christ is 'in no way destroyed through their union' in the one person.

With the Council of Chalcedon, therefore, a touchstone was established for understanding and speaking of Jesus Christ. Justice needs to be done to his divinity. So also, justice is to be done to his humanity. (A later dispute would focus on whether Christ had a human as well as a divine will, and would be resolved to the effect that he had both.) Also, the qualities of both natures having been secured, is the unity of the person preserved? In their images and

---

60   For a contemporary reading of this basic confession of Christian faith, see Kelly, A. J. 1996, *The Creed by Heart: Re-learning the Nicene Creed*, HarperCollins Religious, Blackburn, Victoria.

conceptions of Jesus, Christians over the centuries have been faced with the challenge of maintaining this balance as they have tried 'to think through afresh what God [means] if Jesus Christ [is] intrinsic to who God is, and what it [means] to be human if the criterion of true humanity is Jesus Christ'.[61]

The account that has been given so far—drawing on scripture and early church teaching as it has, however these might be interpreted—for the most part represents a common heritage of those churches that continue to bear the name 'Christian' today. Despite the deep doctrinal divisions that subsequently occurred between different Christian traditions, and the distinctive cultural and theological emphases that have come to mark them, almost all could at least recognise their origins in this scriptural and traditional bedrock.

Inter-religious dialogue

Since the onset of the Enlightenment in the seventeenth century, rationalism and non-belief have constituted a major challenge to the intellectual credibility of the Christian churches, especially in the West. Today, however, an equally, if not more fundamental task for Christians is understanding, relating to and collaborating with adherents of religious traditions other than Christianity—some of which are present in large numbers even in the midst of traditionally Christian societies. Inter-religious dialogue, and the indispensable contribution it has to make to the crucial dialogue of civilisations, has emerged as a major pathway to peace in the twenty-first century.

For a large part of the history of the Christian churches, the attitude towards people of other religious beliefs tended to be determined by a narrow and exclusivist reading of Jesus's portrayal of himself as reported in the Gospel of John: 'I am the way, and the truth, and the life. No one comes to the Father expect through me.'[62] This, combined with the assertion attributed to Peter by the Acts of the Apostles[63] that 'there is no other name under heaven given among mortals by which we must be saved', led Christians in general to take a very poor view of the beliefs and practices of others, not to mention the prospects for non-Christians of being saved (as Christians construed salvation). A more ample reading of the Christian scriptures, however, should give pause for thought It is true that 1 Timothy 2:5 holds that 'there is one mediator between God and

---

61   Ford, *Theology*, p. 102.
62   John 14:6.
63   4:12.

humankind, Christ Jesus, himself human', but this principle must be kept in balance with what precedes it—namely, that God our Saviour 'desires everyone to be saved and to come to the knowledge of the truth'.[64]

Moreover, it has been argued that the verses in the prologue to John's gospel, which have been interpreted conventionally as referring precisely to the historical incarnation of the Word in the humanity of Jesus Christ, could in fact be read as signalling a personal relationship between *all* humankind and the Word *before* the incarnation. 'The true light that, by coming into the world, enlightens everyone'[65] would, in this reading, refer to the pre-incarnation activity of the Word.

A similar argument could be made for a continuation of this same activity of the Word *after* Jesus's resurrection. This is not to detract from the firm Christian belief in the uniqueness of Jesus Christ as universal Saviour, but it does leave scope for a much more positive, appreciative and irenic Christian understanding of the beliefs and practices of others.[66] As the World Council of Churches World Mission Conference meeting in San Antonio in 1989 expressed it: 'We cannot point to any other way of salvation than Jesus Christ; at the same time we cannot set limits to the saving power of God.'

As far as the Roman Catholic Church is concerned, the Second Vatican Council spoke in numerous positive ways of other religious traditions. It acknowledged the 'truth and grace [that] are to be found among the nations' and the 'good [that] is found to be sown in the hearts and minds of men, or in the rites and cultures peculiar to various peoples'.[67]

Seeds of the Word lie hidden there.[68] With specific reference to religious and monastic life, its practitioners are urged to reflect on how they 'might be able to assimilate the ascetic and contemplative traditions, whose seeds were sometimes planted by God in ancient cultures already prior to the preaching of the Gospel'.[69] This will be of particular relevance to the dialogue with Buddhists.

---

64   1 Timothy 2:4.
65   John 1:9.
66   See Dupuis, J. 2002, *Christianity and the Religions: From confrontation to dialogue*, Orbis Books, Maryknoll, NY, pp. 142–4. See also from The World Council of Churches (1990, *The Baar Statement: Theological perspectives on plurality*, accessed 24 September 2009, <http://www.oikoumene.org/en/resources/documents/wcc-programmes/interreligious-dialogue-and-cooperation/christian-identity-in-pluralistic-societies/baar-statement-theological-perspectives-on-plurality.html>): 'This conviction that God as creator of all is present and active in the plurality of religions makes it inconceivable to us that God's saving activity could be confined to any one continent, cultural type, or groups of peoples. A refusal to take seriously the many and diverse religious testimonies to be found among the nations and peoples of the whole world amounts to disowning the biblical testimony to God as creator of all things and father of humankind.'
67   Second Vatican Council 1965, '*Ad* Gentes', Decree on the Mission Activity of the Church, Documents of the II Vatican Council, Holy See, Vatican City, 9.
68   Ibid., 11.
69   Ibid., 18.

Of non-Christian religions in general, the council states:

> The Catholic Church rejects nothing that is true and holy in these religions. She regards with sincere reverence those ways of conduct and life, those precepts and teachings which, though differing in many aspects from the ones she holds and sets forth, nonetheless often reflect a ray of that Truth which enlightens all men.[70]

In the light of this, Catholics are exhorted 'through dialogue and collaboration with followers of other religions…[to] recognise, preserve and promote the good things, spiritual and moral, as well as the socio-cultural values found among these men'. This dialogue can take different forms: the dialogue of life that arises when people share their common human concerns, the dialogue of collaborative action, the dialogue of theological study and exchange, and the dialogue of religious experience.

The dialogue of religious experience is defined as occurring 'where persons, rooted in their own religious traditions, share their spiritual riches, for instance with regard to prayer and contemplation, faith and ways of searching for God or the Absolute'.[71] Specifically in the relationship between Christians and Buddhists, paradigmatic of such dialogue—and an exemplary extension of what had been urged by the Second Vatican Council—are the three Gethsemani Encounters. The first was published under a title that emphasised the centrality of the dialogue of religious experience: *The Gethsemani Encounter: A dialogue on the spiritual life by Buddhist and Christian monastics* (1999). The second and third Gethsemani Encounters have moved as well into the dialogues of action and theological exchange. The second was published under the title *Transforming Suffering: Reflections on finding peace in troubled times* (2002), while the third, which was held in May 2008, addressed the theme 'Monasticism and the environment'.

These encounters, which are sponsored by Monastic Inter-religious Dialogue, represent the culmination of decades of preparation, stemming significantly from the three-day meeting at Dharamsala in 1968 between the Catholic Cistercian monk Thomas Merton and His Holiness the Dalai Lama.

---

70   Second Vatican Council 1965, '*Nostra* Aetate', Declaration on the Relation of the Church to Non-Christian Religions, Documents of the II Vatican Council, Holy See, Vatican City, 28 October, 2.
71   Pontifical Council for Interreligious Dialogue and Congregation for the Evangelization of Peoples 1991, *Dialogue and Proclamation,* Holy See, Vatican City, para. 42.

Conclusion

This presentation of Christianity has taken a predominantly theological approach, focusing largely on the formative period in which most of the churches that go by the name of 'Christian' continue to recognise their own origins. Credal statements and formulas have been highlighted, emphasising that the cognitive dimension plays an important role in the way in which Christian faith has developed. This emphasis on knowing is paralleled by the focus on orthodoxy—understood as right teaching—which has marked the history of the Christian churches. In this way, Christians affirm, for example, the resurrection of the dead, the doctrine of the Holy Trinity and even that 'God is love'.

As well as exploring the meaning of the doctrines that they learn and are taught, however, Christians find that their very identity as human beings is radically affected by the faith they proclaim. Faith in the risen Christ has radical implications for the way they understand and live out their own humanity, for they have been called to glory in light of the resurrection promise that 'this mortal body must put on immortality'.[72] The Holy Trinity is also therefore not just the specifically Christian way of speaking about God, it is the very mystery of love that dwells in believers, making them sons and daughters of God, members of Christ and temples of the Holy Spirit.

Third, the meaning of being Christian, while including knowledge of what is taught by the Church and the shaping of personal identity, is also essentially communitarian. The resurrection of Jesus culminates in the sending of the Holy Spirit at Pentecost by which divisions between people are overcome and the Christian community begins to take shape.[73] Similarly, the Holy Trinity, as an exchange of divine relationships, opens human beings and the world to a dynamic and fruitful sharing in the communion that is the very life of God, who is love.

Finally, countless examples could be offered of how Christian faith has been effective—that is, how Christians have made meaning of their faith—for the good of the world. Tertullian's observation from the end of the first century—'see how these Christians love one another'[74]—was at least an indication that the injunction of 1 John 3:18 to 'love not in word or speech, but in truth and action' was being heeded in Christian communities. Now, however, it is increasingly clear that Christianity being an effective positive force in the world of the future will depend in large measure on the capacity of its loving, which is grounded in God as love, to manifest itself in continuing and deepening dialogue with those of other religious traditions. In this enterprise, however, Christianity's

---

72 1 Corinthians 15:53.
73 Acts 2:1–13.
74 Tertullian *197*, Apologeticum, 39.7.

best contribution will surely flow from fidelity to its own deepest experiences of, and insights into, the Creator God, His Son, Jesus Christ, who died on the cross and was raised from the dead, the Holy Spirit of God poured out on the world, the Church as a communion of life with God and with one another, and the eternal life of the world to come. In stressing the movement between Father, Son and Holy Spirit, this Triune Christianity is marked profoundly by the refusal to allow its account of God's nature and action to be finally and exclusively tied down to one alone of Father, Son or Holy Spirit. Much less does it permit Christians to think that in their conceptual constructs they have really comprehended God. They might hope, therefore, that the transcendent openness and newness of the Triune God can still create fresh clearings for the free and purposeful dialogue that will extend us all.

Select bibliography

Hart, D. B. 2007, *The Story of Christianity: An illustrated history of 2000 years of the Christian faith*, Quercus, London.

Lefebure, L. D. 1993, The *Buddha and the Christ: Explorations in Buddhist and Christian dialogue*, Orbis Books, Maryknoll, NY.

Macmillan, G. 2004, *Understanding Christianity*, Dunedin Academic Press, Edinburgh.

Pieris, A., S. J. 1988, *Love Meets Wisdom: A Christian experience of Buddhism*, Orbis Books, Maryknoll, NY.

Ward, K. 2000, *Christianity: A short introduction*, Oneworld, Oxford.

Woodhead, L. 2004, *Christianity: A very short introduction*, Oxford University Press, Oxford.

9. Introduction to Buddhism
PROFESSOR JOHN POWERS,
THE AUSTRALIAN NATIONAL UNIVERSITY

Buddhism is one of the world's major religions, with adherents on every continent except Antarctica. Gauging the total number of contemporary Buddhists is highly problematic and depends on what criteria one uses. About 400 million people have taken formal refuge vows and so have demonstrated a commitment to the tradition, but according to some estimates there could be as many as 1.5 billion Buddhists worldwide, whose real level of adherence or knowledge of the tradition ranges from fervent devotion to a weak sense of connection through family histories.

An added difficulty in determining numbers of Buddhists is related to the fact that some substantial Buddhist populations exist in countries such as China whose governments are strongly opposed to religion. This leads some followers to deny membership even when they privately consider themselves Buddhists, and official statistics tend to undervalue religious adherents in all traditions.

The Buddha

The founder of Buddhism was a prince named Siddhartha Gautama, who was born into a royal family in what is today southern Nepal, probably about the third or fourth century BCE. He made no claim to originality and instead declared that he had rediscovered and revived an ancient tradition that had also been proclaimed by previous buddhas. According to traditional accounts, he was exceptionally gifted and shortly after his birth a group of astrologers gathered to prognosticate about his future.

All agreed that he would become a universal monarch and rule according to truth and righteousness (*dharma*). One astrologer agreed that this might be his destiny, but added that if he were to see four sights before full adulthood, he would pursue another career: he would renounce household life and his wealthy inheritance and become a buddha who would bring countless living beings to salvation.

The four sights were: 1) an old man; 2) a sick man; 3) a corpse; and 4) a world-renouncing ascetic. The first three represent the most pervasive problems of existence: all beings suffer from illness from time to time, all grow old and experience the debilitating effects of senescence, and all eventually die, a process that is generally accompanied by physical and emotional pain. The fourth sight indicates a way to escape from this fate, one that involves turning one's back on the purported pleasures of the world and pursuing a difficult path that leads to liberation.

Cyclic existence

According to Buddhism, all beings are born over and over in a beginning-less process. Each life is conditioned by the volitional actions (*karma*) of one's past lives and present actions will similarly determine the important aspects of future life situations. Every action one performs leads to an opposite and equal reaction either in the present life or in future ones. Those who engage in evil acts might be reborn as animals that suffer and die early or as hell beings whose bodies are designed to experience excruciating pain without let-up. Beings who cultivate good qualities such as generosity, compassion and equanimity may enjoy lives as well-favoured humans or even as gods in one of the various heavens described in Buddhist cosmology.

All conditions, however, are impermanent (*anitya*). Hell beings suffer for a long time, but eventually work off their negative karma and move on to less unpleasant situations. Gods think that their perfect bodies, unlimited resources and perfectly happy lives will last forever, but in fact they are living on past good deeds; when these are exhausted, the former gods fall to one of the lower realms of cyclic existence.

Most beings are completely unaware of the operations of the system and so tend to engage in actions that will have negative consequences. This ignorance (*avidya*) is a core element of the system and the primary factor that keeps it going. Most beings see evidence of pervasive suffering but ignore it and pursue transient pleasures such as money, fame, sex and power, not realising that they will eventually be lost, along with one's body and life.

The Buddha's renunciation

The Buddha's father, King Shuddhodana, was determined that his son would never encounter the negative aspects of cyclic existence before he became fully committed to his royal destiny. The king ordered that only young, healthy people be allowed in the palace and that if anyone died the corpse should be removed before Siddhartha could see it. The prince was kept cloistered within the palace walls, surrounded by scores of beautiful women whose only goal was to keep him happy. He engaged in sporting events and martial arts contests with other young men and he always bested his opponents. His father ensured that he had the best that a wealthy kingdom could offer.

When Siddhartha reached young adulthood, his father arranged a marriage with the beautiful Yashodhara, and she soon conceived a son. By this time, however, Siddhartha was beginning to have profound doubts about his life and yearned to find ultimate salvation. Recognising that family ties were an impediment to the religious quest, he named the infant Rahula (Fetter).

Siddhartha began to wonder what life was like beyond the palace walls. His father tried to dissuade him, but Siddhartha insisted that as a future king he needed to see his kingdom and interact with his subjects. The king reluctantly agreed to let Siddhartha view the capital city, Kapilavastu, in his royal chariot, but first ordered that the route be cleared of all old and sick people, that no funerals approach that area and that all ascetics be banned from the city.

Despite Shuddhodana's efforts, the chariot was soon stopped by a frail, sick man who hobbled painfully across the street. Siddhartha, who had never encountered illness of any kind, was shocked by the man's condition and asked his charioteer how he came to be this way. The prince was informed that sickness could strike anyone at any time and that all people inevitably experienced it. Shocked to learn that his young, healthy body might some day degenerate like that of the sick man, Siddhartha ordered that the chariot return to the palace so that he could contemplate this new insight.

On subsequent trips, he saw an old man and a corpse accompanied by friends and relatives wailing and lamenting, and thus he became fully aware of the realities of cyclic existence. On his fourth trip, he saw a world-renouncing ascetic standing apart from the crowds, a smile on his lips and his body proclaiming attainment of inner peace. Siddhartha asked his charioteer about the man, and on being informed that he was a solitary seeker of religious truth, the prince decided then and there that he would emulate the ascetic's example and become one of the multitude of homeless wanderers who roamed India in search of liberation from cyclic existence.

When Siddhartha returned to the palace and informed his father, the king saw that all his efforts to keep his son immersed in the world had failed. Though his father redoubled his efforts to beguile him with worldly pleasures, the young prince had lost all taste for them. One night after a wild revel, he decided to leave the palace and make his way to the edge of the wilderness, where wandering ascetics gathered to practise austerities, engage in meditation and share insights on ways to detach themselves from the round of birth, death and rebirth.

He left behind his loving wife and young son, renounced his royal inheritance and cast aside any lingering attachments to material things: 'In the spring of my life, despite the tears shed by my parents, I shaved my head, put on robes, renounced my home, and became a homeless monk.'[1]

Soon afterward, Siddhartha met a meditation master who showed him a technique leading to a blissful meditative state. Although the state appeared to be sublime and free from suffering, Siddhartha realised that it was only temporary and that he could not remain in a trance indefinitely. This practice could not fulfil his quest for a final end to suffering, so he travelled to another teacher, who taught him an even more advanced and blissful meditation technique, but the subsequent experience of trance was also impermanent.

Siddhartha then joined a group of five ascetics who believed that the way to find release from suffering lay in physical austerities. They fasted for long periods, avoided any sort of bodily enjoyment and engaged in practices designed to increase pain. After six years of this regimen—during which Siddhartha came to resemble a skeleton with skin stretched thinly over it—one day he passed out from weakness and hunger. On awakening, he realised that severe asceticism was just as much a hindrance to liberation as his previous hedonistic lifestyle.

This led to one of his great insights, referred to by Buddhists as the 'middle way' (*madhyama-pratipad*), which held that those who pursued liberation must maintain a balance and avoid extreme practices. His ascetic companions, however, decided that Siddhartha was a weakling who lacked the resolve to follow their path, so they left him. Siddhartha was unconcerned, because he fully understood the futility of their practices.

Siddhartha then travelled to Bodh Gaya in modern-day Bihar and fashioned a meditation seat under a tree that would later become known as the 'Tree of Awakening'. Resolving to remain there until he had overcome ignorance and found the path to liberation, Siddhartha entered into progressively more and more blissful meditative states. During the night, he comprehended the 'four noble truths', which would later become core elements of Buddhist philosophy and soteriology: 1) all life involves suffering; 2) suffering has a cause, and this cause is desire; 3) suffering can be overcome; and 4) the way to overcome suffering is through pursuit of the eightfold noble path (1. correct views; 2. correct intentions; 3. correct speech; 4. correct actions; 5. correct livelihood; 6. correct effort; 7. correct mindfulness; and 8. correct concentration). Taken together, these constitute a program for cognitive restructuring that begins with examination of one's views and revising them in accordance with empirical

---

1 Majjhima-nikaya I.163.

evidence and reasoning. This is followed by moral cultivation, which leads to a calm and stable mind. This is the basis for practice of advanced meditation, which eliminates mental afflictions and leads to wisdom.

A key element involves training in mindfulness. One develops keen awareness of one's body, sensations, feelings, thoughts, impulses and the phenomena of the surrounding environment. This training also involves examining one's views and motivations and considering how they influence behaviour. Through this process, one becomes aware of the transitory and fleeting nature of phenomena and of one's mental states and the consequences of one's decisions. Mindfulness is not affected by prejudice, but rather is a clear and accurate analysis that understands the dependently arisen nature of the phenomena of experience.

It helps one to understand the impermanent nature of one's physical processes, experiences, thoughts and emotions and to judge whether they are positive, negative or neutral. Through mindfulness, one recognises the dynamic and changing nature of physical and mental factors—of one's own body and mind and the world.

In the *Exegesis* (*Atthasalini*), the great commentator Buddhaghosa describes it as 'not floating away'. He states that it involves retaining something in one's awareness and not letting one's attention just skim the surface of events. Rather, one becomes aware of physical and mental processes in a dispassionate manner, without passing judgment, fully aware of what is happening but not reacting with habitual tendencies.

Attainment of buddhahood

As the sun rose the next morning, Siddhartha eliminated the final vestiges of ignorance, perfected his understanding and insight and thus became a *buddha* or 'awakened one'. This epithet implied that he no longer viewed the world through the distorted lens of ignorance that caused ordinary beings to pursue counterproductive ends and engage in acts that led to their own suffering. The Buddha fully understood the interdependent nature of the universe: all aspects of reality interacted with everything else and phenomena were characterised by relations of mutual conditioning and influence.

At first, the Buddha thought that what he had realised was far too profound for ordinary beings to grasp, but on further reflection he decided that there were some people whose perceptions were only thinly clouded and who might grasp the import of his insights and thus attain nirvana—the final cessation of suffering. He decided to travel to Varanasi, where his five former companions were still engaging in fruitless austerities, and he delivered a sermon now commonly referred to as 'the discourse turning the wheel of dharma'. He chided his former companions for their excessive attachment to asceticism and advised them to follow the middle way:

> O monks, these two extremes should not be practiced by one who has gone forth [from the homeless life]. What are the two? That which is linked with sensual desires—which is low, vulgar, common, unworthy, and useless—and that which is linked with self-torture—which is painful, unworthy, and useless. By avoiding these two extremes, the Tathagata [Buddha] has gained the knowledge of the middle path which gives vision and knowledge and leads to calm, to clairvoyances, to awakening, to nirvana.[2]

He expounded the four noble truths, the eightfold noble path and interdependent origination. All five ascetics had profound realisations and one became an *arhat*, meaning that he would attain nirvana at the end of his life.

The monastic community

The five ascetics became the first Buddhist monks. The monastic order was seen by the Buddha as the bedrock of the Buddhist community and even today people wishing to enter the faith vow to take refuge in the *samgha* (the order of ordained monks and nuns). They also take refuge in the Buddha and the doctrine (*dharma*) and only people who have formally made this declaration are generally considered fully committed members of the community.

As the Buddha travelled and taught, he attracted a large number of followers. He soon instituted an order of nuns for women seeking full-time religious vocations. A number of wealthy lay patrons donated land for the use of the *samgha*, and on some of this the first Buddhist monastic structures were built. The Buddha travelled and taught for 40 years and eventually died at the age of eighty. In his final instructions, he advised his followers to pursue their own salvations with diligence and said that the collected teachings he had delivered should be their guide. He then passed into nirvana.

After the death of the Buddha, the monastic order he founded continued the traditions he established. He did not name a successor and the *samgha* adopted a democratic form of management in which disputes were decided by a majority of fully ordained monks. Their peers judged members who transgressed the rules and punishments were meted out in accordance with a corpus of rules attributed to the Buddha (the *Vinaya*).

---

2   Samyutta-nikaya V.420–3.

Disputes soon began to arise concerning exactly what the Buddha had taught, and within a few decades of his death, the 'First Buddhist Council' was convened in Rajagrha to settle the matter. A group of 500 *arhats* recounted from memory his discourses and teachings on monastic discipline. These became the first two 'baskets' (*pitaka*) of the Buddhist canon. Later, a third basket containing scholastic teachings attributed to the Buddha was added. During the first council, the Buddha's attendant, Ananda, who had been present for most of his public teachings, repeated what he had heard and other members of the assembly either agreed or made minor corrections. Upali, the master of the *Vinaya*, recounted the Buddha's rules for monastic life. At the conclusion of the council, the canon was declared closed. Only material approved by the council of *arhats* would count as the 'word of the Buddha'. The three baskets were codified in a language called Pali, so this collection was commonly referred to as the 'Pali canon'.

Mahayana

Despite the canonising aspirations of the first council, new discourses claiming to have been spoken by the Buddha continued to appear, and some groups within the tradition regarded them as authentic.

The most significant and influential body of new scriptures was the 'Perfection of Wisdom Discourses', which began to appear about the first century CE. In the earliest of these, the *8,000 Line Perfection of Wisdom Discourse*, there is a significant shift in doctrine and practice. The Buddha declares that his earlier discourses were merely expedient teachings delivered to followers of inferior capacities. They were not incorrect, and he does not deny the validity of the four noble truths, dependent arising and other core doctrines, but they are now interpreted in light of new concepts and the Buddhist path is radically reconceived.

In the Pali canon, the ideal practitioner is the *arhat*, who eliminates mental afflictions such as anger, desire and obscuration, who cultivates advanced meditative states and attains nirvana at the culmination of the path. This process begins with 'stream entry', an existential transformation that establishes a person on the path and requires at least three human lifetimes to complete. *Arhats* are said to have compassion for the sufferings of others and they provide teachings and examples for their benefit, but their primary goal is nirvana for themselves alone.

In the Pali canon, *arhats* are portrayed as heroic figures, but in the Perfection of Wisdom Discourses they are lambasted as selfish people who pursue only a limited path for their own benefit. The new dispensation refers to itself as the

'Great Vehicle' (*Mahayana*) and characterises rival systems as belonging to an 'Inferior Vehicle' (*Hinayana*) whose adherents pay insufficient attention to the sufferings of others. In Mahayana literature, the paradigmatic practitioner is the *bodhisattva*, who strives to attain buddhahood in order to benefit all sentient beings.

The bodhisattva is motivated by compassion. The Mahayana path begins with a growing realisation of the pervasiveness of suffering and the infinite numbers of sentient beings who go from birth to birth committing actions based on ignorance that will lead to negative consequences in the future. Contemplating in this way, a practitioner with a high level of compassion and intelligence spontaneously generates the 'mind of awakening' (*bodhicitta*), a profound existential transformation after which he or she is motivated primarily by the sufferings of others and a wish to help them attain happiness. At this point one becomes a *bodhisattva* and thus pursues a path that involves mainly training in the six perfections (*paramita*: generosity, ethics, patience, effort, concentration and wisdom), which when cultivated to their ultimate level become the core aspects of the awakened personality of a buddha. The time required to complete the path from the moment of *bodhicitta* is said to be a minimum of three 'countless eons' (the amount of time between the creation and destruction of the universe), so only practitioners with unusually strong compassion will succeed.

One of the most important aspects of the *bodhisattva*'s motivation is a profound realisation of emptiness (*shunyata*): all phenomena utterly lack any substantial essence and everything is composed of parts brought together by causes and conditions. This applies to people, who lack any enduring essence or soul, and to non-sentient things, which are similarly conceived by Buddhism as dependent arisings that come into being, change from moment to moment and eventually pass away.

A person who thoroughly grasps the utter absence of self or essence does not feel any loss; rather, this is a profoundly liberating understanding that frees one from the shackles of egoistic thinking and grasping after possessions. When *bodhisattvas* eliminate the false notion of self—initially through a process of reasoning that is subsequently deepened by meditative internalisation of this insight—they find that the natural concern for oneself no longer has any artificial, self-imposed boundaries. Compassion and concern extend outward. The entire universe is intertwined in bonds of mutual influence and *bodhisattvas* who directly cognise emptiness naturally feel the same concern for others as for themselves.

As Mahayana developed in India, new philosophical schools emerged. The two most influential were the Middle Way School (*Madhyamaka*)—which based itself on the Perfection of Wisdom Discourses and emphasised the use of dialectical reasoning in overcoming false views, developing cognitive clarity and perfecting insight—and the Yogic Practice School (*Yogacara*), which criticised its rival's emphasis on reasoning and asserted the centrality of introspective meditation in the path to liberation.

Tantric Buddhism

In the latter half of the seventh century, a third wave of texts claiming canonical status began to appear in India. Many of these contained the term '*tantra*' (continuum) in their titles, and thus this corpus was commonly referred to as 'Tantra'. The general outlines of the tantric path accord with those of previous Mahayana systems: the *bodhisattva* is the ideal figure, the goal of practice is attainment of buddhahood for the benefit of other sentient beings and the *bodhisattva* cultivates the six perfections during the course of training.

Despite these similarities, there are also significant differences. Tantric Buddhism emphasises the use of imagery and ritual as part of the cognitive restructuring involved in transitioning from the mind-set of an ordinary being to that of a buddha. Tantric texts describe symbolic diagrams (*mandala*) that serve as templates for this mental transformation. Mandalas commonly have a round border and often have a four-sided palace in the centre, which represents the dwelling of the central buddha of its rituals and meditations. The mandala incorporates symbolism that reflects Buddhist doctrines and practices, and by turning one's attention to it over and over, one subliminally reorients one's cognitions and perceptions.

Tantric texts claim that their special techniques can greatly shorten the training period and that particularly gifted trainees can become buddhas in as little as one human lifetime.

Tantric meditation emphasises the importance of familiarisation of the mind with an object of observation. The more one internalises a mandala, symbolic physical gestures (*mudra*) or mantras, the more one's mind becomes transformed in accordance with their symbolism. Tantra theory holds that Hinayana and mainstream Mahayana are slow paths to liberation because they use mainly techniques that are concordant with the goal, but tantra is faster, more powerful and more effective because its practitioners train directly at being buddhas, so they attain this state more quickly than is possible with other systems.

A core practice of this system is deity yoga (*devata-yoga*), in which trainees repeatedly generate a vivid image of a buddha and imagine themselves transforming into that awakened being. They imagine that they have the body, speech and mind of a buddha and become familiar with performing the compassionate deeds associated with buddhahood.

Tantric practice generally begins with a formal initiation ceremony, in which a fully qualified master introduces students to the symbolism of a particular mandala associated with a tantric buddha. During the ceremony, students take vows of utter commitment to the practice and promise not to reveal it to others who are not 'suitable vessels'. Tantric Buddhism places a high value on secrecy and holds that only trainees with the highest capacities are worthy of being introduced to its mysteries. Tantric practice is not possible without initiation and anyone who pretends to practice tantra without it is merely deluded.

After initiation, one generally is assigned a regular practice of a liturgy of chanting and visualisation (*sadhana*). One becomes part of a community and is urged to regard others with the same initiation and lineage as '*vajra* brothers and sisters'. The *vajra* is the core symbol of tantric Buddhism, which is often referred to as the '*Vajra* Vehicle' (*Vajrayana*). A *vajra* is a five-pronged sceptre that represents a royal staff from medieval India. It symbolises an unbreakable substance and is associated with the profound combination of perfected wisdom and compassion that characterises the mind of a buddha.

Tantric Buddhism emphasises the non-differentiability of cyclic existence and nirvana. From the perspective of a buddha, there is no difference; sentient beings imagine that their deluded perceptions correspond with reality, but in fact they are profoundly coloured by the distorting lenses of ignorance, desire, anger, greed and obscuration, which superimpose a false overlay on mental phenomena. All of our perceptions are interpreted by the mind and no-one ever cognises things directly without the mediation of consciousness.

Ordinary beings therefore live in a world that appears to them through a distorting lens, while buddhas who have eliminated all mental faults perceive reality as it is. Both groups, however, direct their attention towards the same things—the only difference is their respective mentalities. When one completely removes cognitive affliction and perfects wisdom and compassion to their highest levels, one is a buddha, but the world never changes, only one's perceptions of it.

Tantric Buddhist meditation theory assumes a notion found in the Pali canon and developed further in Mahayana literature—that the mind is of the essence of clear light (*prabhasvara-citta*). All afflictions are adventitious (*agantuka*)—that is, they are not of the nature of the mind, so they can be eliminated. Buddhism has no concept of a 'fall' in which beings become mentally afflicted; we have suffered from the distorting effects of mental defilements since beginning-less time, and they have promoted negative behaviour, but they can be eliminated through meditative practice and cultivation of virtue. Once afflictions are eliminated, there is no basis for their return because they are antithetical to the clear-light nature of the mind. At a certain point, a *bodhisattva* becomes 'irreversible', meaning that there is no possibility of backsliding. From this point, progress towards buddhahood is steady and one gradually perfects good qualities while simultaneously eliminating remaining subtle traces of mental affliction.

Demise of Buddhism in India

Production of tantras continued for several centuries, and reports from the eighth century onwards indicated that they rapidly gained popularity and became an integral part of the curriculum of the great monastic universities of northern India that were the main seats of Buddhist training and practice. At the same time, small groups of tantric adepts (*siddha*) developed, mainly in the northern Indian states of Bihar and Bengal, which often challenged the institutionalised tantric practice of the monasteries. Adepts such as Tilopa and Naropa ridiculed the pretensions of academic Buddhists and claimed that their own teachings and techniques were far more advanced and effective. These two streams continued to grow and develop, sometimes borrowing from each other and sometimes engaging in polemics, until the demise of Buddhism in the twelfth and thirteenth centuries, and they were also transmitted to Tibet.

Buddhism's decline and disappearance were due to a number of factors, including a decrease in patronage, shifting demographics and perennially small numbers in contrast with those of the dominant Brahmanical tradition. The main factor, though, was a series of Muslim invasions from the north, which targeted institutions of other religions. Because Buddhism traditionally enjoyed a close relationship with merchants, many of its major establishments were built near trade routes. These were the main routes followed by the Muslim armies, which engaged in widespread destruction, pillaging and slaughter.

The great monastic universities of Nalanda and Vikramasila were sacked and many of their residents killed, and as waves of invaders continued to move into the Subcontinent, they dealt Buddhism a deathblow from which it never recovered. By the end of the thirteenth century, Buddhism existed only in small communities at the periphery of India and had been eliminated from the places of its origin and early flourishing.

The spread of Buddhism

Although Buddhism died out in the land of its origin, it spread widely throughout Asia, and today is gaining converts all over the world. In the United States and Australia, census data indicate that Buddhism is the fastest-growing religion. This is due to a combination of migration from traditional Buddhist countries and conversion of people born into non-Buddhist communities.

According to tradition, the Indian King Ashoka instituted the first Buddhist mission in the third century CE. He sent his son, Mahinda, a Buddhist monk, to the island of Sri Lanka, along with a quorum of other fully ordained monks and his sister, Sanghamitta, a Buddhist nun. Mahinda's mission was reportedly highly successful and the king of the island, Devanampiya Tissa, converted to Buddhism along with the royal court. He provided funds to build the first Buddhist monastery, the Mahavihara. This became the seat of Buddhist orthodoxy in Sri Lanka for more than a millennium. Soon, Sri Lankans began to enter the monastic order and a lineage of nuns was also established.

The dominant school of Buddhism in Sri Lanka today is Theravada, whose name translates as 'Teachings of the Elders'. It prides itself on its conservatism and portrays itself as the most orthodox of all Buddhist traditions. Its scriptural source is the Pali canon, which it believes contains the entire 'word of the Buddha', and it rejects Mahayana as a false system whose scriptures are apocryphal. Despite this stance, one of the most striking features of contemporary Buddhism in Sri Lanka is its syncretism: most Buddhist establishments have Hindu shrines and images, and much of the daily practice of avowed Buddhists is indistinguishable from that of Hindus. They worship Hindu deities and propitiate them for worldly benefits, but also proclaim a primary commitment to Buddhism.

In Theravada, the Buddha is generally conceived as utterly transcendent, so there is no point in praying to him to cure illness, provide a better job or for aid during times of misfortune. For such matters, one turns towards worldly deities. It is generally assumed in Theravada countries that it is possible to attain liberation from cyclic existence only during the time of a buddha, so most Buddhists—monks and laypeople—devote themselves to merit-making activities in the hope that they might be born during the time of the future buddha, Maitreya, in a life situation that is conducive to the pursuit of nirvana.

Sri Lanka remained a lone Theravada outpost until the twelfth century, when Theravada was transmitted to Thailand. In the fifteenth century, Theravada was established in Cambodia and it soon spread to neighbouring countries, including Laos and Burma. It remains the dominant tradition of Buddhism in South-East Asia today.

East Asia

Beginning in the first century CE, Buddhism began to move eastwards from India, following the trade routes that connected China with the Indian Subcontinent. Buddhist monarchs ruled several of the major oasis cities along the Silk Routes and a number of missionary monks travelled to China to spread the dharma. One of the most influential of these was An Shigao, who arrived in the Chinese capital of Changan in 145 and established a translation bureau. Together with other Central Asian monks, he translated a range of Buddhist scriptures into Chinese, but during this period Buddhism was generally regarded as a foreign religion and had few Chinese adherents.

Many of the early translators adopted the practice of 'matching concepts' (*keyi*), which involved using traditional Chinese philosophical terms for Sanskrit words. This helped them in making Buddhism appear more familiar to Chinese readers, but inevitably introduced shifts in meaning. An example is the translation of 'nirvana' with the Daoist term '*wuwei*', meaning 'non-action'. This is the approach of the Daoist sage, who moves in accordance with the rhythms of nature and does not force changes. It does not suggest elimination of the three primary mental afflictions of Indian Buddhist meditation theory, nor does it reflect the mind-set of an *arhat* as traditionally understood in India. The technique of matching concepts had the desired effect of making Buddhist terminology appear less foreign to Chinese readers, but inevitably led to significant doctrinal deviations from Indian Buddhism.

One of the most significant of these was a widespread belief among early Chinese Buddhists that Buddhism asserted the existence of a soul. They thought that this was necessitated by the doctrine of rebirth, but as we have seen, the Buddha denied the existence of a soul and viewed reincarnation as a process in which a constantly changing psychophysical continuum moved to a new body and began a new life.

When the Buddhist monk Kumarajiva (344–413) arrived in China, he worked to overturn such misguided notions and advocated literal translations for technical Sanskrit terms. He had a profound influence on the subsequent development of Chinese Buddhism, but the tradition continued to develop in ways significantly different from its Indian origins. As in other countries to which it travelled, Buddhism adapted itself to local customs and incorporated indigenous deities and even demonic forces. Folk beliefs and customs were refigured in a Buddhist guise and at the same time advanced philosophical systems developed.

Buddhism began to attract Chinese converts during the Western Jin (256–316) and Eastern Jin (317–419) periods, and some took monastic ordination. During subsequent dynasties, Buddhism began to spread widely, initially among mainly the educated aristocracy, who were attracted by its large corpus of philosophical literature and highly developed systems of meditative practice. Another important factor was Buddhism's huge pantheon of compassionate buddhas and *bodhisattvas*, who promised aid to anyone who called on them with faith.

The apogee of Chinese Buddhism was reached during the Tang Dynasty (618–906), but there was a severe crackdown by the government in 845, which led to the destruction of many monasteries and forced a return to lay life for thousands of monastics. Despite this short-lived but violent persecution, Buddhism continued to spread and attract converts. Indigenous schools developed, such as the Pure Land (*Qingtu*) tradition, which sought rebirth in Sukhavati, the heavenly realm of the Buddha Amitabha, through devotional activities, and the Chan (Japanese: Zen) school, which developed a program of meditation designed to lead to a sudden experience of awakening.

Buddhism spread widely among the masses during successive dynasties, and for many Chinese came to be viewed as one component of the 'three traditions' (Confucianism, Daoism and Buddhism), each of which pertained to a particular aspect of one's religious life. When the Communists led by Mao Zedong came to power in 1947, they declared war on religion. Mao characterised religion as 'poison' and during the Cultural Revolution (1966–76), the new government made concerted efforts to eradicate it. In recent decades, there has been a relative relaxation of persecution, which has led to widespread revival of religious practice in China.

Japan

From China, Buddhism spread to Korea, and from there to Japan. The first prominent royal adherent of the new tradition was Prince Shotoku (574–622), who was viewed by later tradition as a *bodhisattva* and who was credited with establishing temples all over the country and composing several influential commentaries on Buddhist texts.

During the Nara Period (710–84), six philosophical schools rose to prominence, and later the Tendai (Chinese: *Tientai*) school was imported from China, along with traditions of tantric Buddhism (*Shingon*) and Chan. During the Kamakura Period (1185–1333), Japanese Buddhists developed indigenous schools. An important figure of this time was the Buddhist priest Nichiren, who trained initially in the scholastic Tendai tradition and later created his own school, which emphasised the centrality of the *Lotus Sutra*.

His followers chant the title of the *sutra* (in Japanese) as a way of invoking the scripture's power, which can be used to acquire worldly benefits and to promote spiritual advancement.

During the Tokugawa Period (1600–1867), warlords seized power from the central government and Buddhism was declared the state religion. Despite this apparent advantage, Buddhism suffered an overall decline in fortunes because the clergy became lazy and no longer bothered to learn the tradition well enough to explain or defend it. Because they were forced into verbal adherence to Buddhism, laypeople became indifferent and the subsequent Meiji Dynasty (1868–1912) delivered a further blow by making Shinto the state religion and purging Shinto sites of Buddhist statues. After Japan's defeat in World War II, the victorious Allies instituted a system of religious freedom in Japan. Contemporary surveys, however, indicate that the majority of the population is indifferent to religion. Buddhism continues to enjoy widespread support, but for many Japanese this is more a matter of following established family traditions than heartfelt devotion.

Tibet

Buddhism first entered Tibet during the seventh century. According to tradition, King Songtsen Gampo (ca 618–50) played a pivotal role in the 'first dissemination' of Buddhism, along with his two foreign wives—one from Nepal and the other from China. Songtsen Gampo is portrayed as a physical emanation of the buddha Chenrezi (Sanskrit: *Avalokiteshvara*) in traditional sources, and his two foreign brides are incarnations of the buddha Tara. The three consciously took rebirth in Tibet intending to play definitive roles in establishing Buddhism there.

Despite this pious story, there is no contemporaneous evidence that Songtsen Gampo had any real interest in Buddhism and there are no accounts of any pro-Buddhist activities initiated by him. Tibetan tradition, however, regards him as the first of Tibet's 'religious kings'. His successor, Tri Songdetsen (ca 740–98), was by all accounts a devout Buddhist, and dynastic records indicated that he devoted significant resources to propagating the faith.

Tibetan histories reported that during Tri Songdetsen's reign, interest in Buddhism increased all over the Tibetan cultural area, and masters from India and China travelled widely, propagating a range of divergent systems. This led to conflicts between different paradigms of practice and doctrine, and in 792, the king decided to stage a winner-take-all debate between leading factions advocating Indian and Chinese models. The main proponent of the traditional

Indian gradualist paradigm was Kamalashila, while the Chinese faction was led by the Chan master Heshang Moheyan, who advocated an antinomian approach to Buddhist ethics and championed the paradigm of 'sudden awakening'.

He claimed that all beings had an inherent 'buddha nature' and that practice involved authenticating this rather than newly cultivating qualities one lacked, such as wisdom, compassion, generosity, and so forth. Practise of ethics is useless as long as one is on the path because one can become a buddha at any moment by ceasing to cling to thoughts. When one has become a buddha, one transcends ordinary ethics.

Kamalashila and his faction argued that nothing—including attainment of buddhahood—happened instantly. Rather, one must follow the path step by step and acquire a range of good qualities that will become the matrix of the awakened personality of a buddha. They demanded that the Chinese side produce examples corroborating their theories, which they were unable to do. According to traditional Tibetan histories, the Chinese were reduced to silence and Kamalashila's side was declared victorious. In accordance with the rules of the debate, the Chinese monks withdrew from Tibet and were forbidden from preaching their doctrine. Heshang Moheyan later avenged his humiliation by hiring Chinese assassins, who travelled to Tibet and murdered Kamalashila by squeezing his kidneys.

There is considerable debate among modern scholars regarding the historicity of the debate, and a general consensus has arisen that it probably never occurred—at least in the form depicted in histories written by Buddhist clerics—but it is widely accepted by Tibetan Buddhists, and the main lesson they derive from it is the conclusion that Chinese Buddhism is heretical while Indian Buddhism is normative.

Support for Buddhism reached its apogee during the reign of the third 'religious king', Relpachen (r. 815–36), but he prompted a backlash by devoting lavish funding to its propagation. In addition, he required that every monk be supported by seven households, even those with no interest in or devotion towards Buddhism. This sparked a revolt by his ministers and led to his assassination. He was succeeded by Lang Darma (r. 838–42), who was assassinated by a Buddhist monk angered at his persecution of Buddhism. This led to the collapse of the imperial dynasty, and for several centuries afterward there was no person or group with the power to rule Tibet.

In the eleventh century, a revival of Buddhism began, sparked by patronage by kings of the kingdom of Guge in western Tibet and the activities of the great translator Rinchen Sangpo, who travelled to India to study and returned in 798. During the same period, monks from eastern Tibet who had maintained the monastic discipline during the interregnum began to ordain monks from the central provinces, and the combined efforts of these groups and individuals inaugurated the 'second dissemination'. Indian scholars, including the renowned master Atisha (982–1054), were invited to Tibet, and Tibetan students were sent to the great northern Indian monastic universities to study.

Atisha's disciple Dromdön (1008–64) founded the Kadampa order, which emphasised a combination of scholastic study, monastic discipline and tantric practice. It was later revived by Tsong Khapa (1357–1419), whose order was initially called the 'New Kadampa' and later came to be known as *Gelukpa* ('System of Virtue'). Other indigenous orders include: 1) the *Nyingmapa* ('Old Order'), which traces its origins to the first dissemination and relies mainly on translations of tantras from that period; 2) the *Kagyüpa* ('Teaching Lineage'), whose origins lie in tantric lineages from Bengal and Bihar; and 3) the *Sakyapa* ('Grey Earth'), named after the site of its first monastery. These orders remain the most important in contemporary Tibetan Buddhism. The Kagyüpa, Sakyapa and Gelukpa are referred to collectively as 'New Orders' (*Sarma*) because they rely mainly on translations of tantras prepared during the second dissemination.

The Sakyapas became the political leaders of Tibet after the region's annexation by the Mongols during the twelfth century. The Mongols also conquered China during this period, but when their power waned during the thirteenth century, Tibet and China regained their independence. The People's Republic of China claims that Tibet became an 'inalienable' part of China as a result of incorporation into the Mongol Empire, but this is historically untenable. Tibet and China were conquered territories in a vast empire that stretched across most of Asia and included large parts of Eastern Europe. Using the same logic, Australia could claim India as an inalienable part of its territory because both were part of the British Empire. Moreover, if China's territorial claim to Tibet were legitimate, it would have an equally valid right to ownership of Lithuania, Korea and Iran— all of which were also conquered by the Mongols and annexed to their empire.

After Tibet reverted to indigenous rule, various local and regional potentates emerged, but none was able to unify the country until the fifth Dalai Lama, Ngawang Losang Gyatso (1617–82), did so with the help of the Mongol ruler Gushri Khan in the seventeenth century. From this point onwards, his successors (or their regents) were at least nominal rulers of Tibet for most of the period until 1959, when the fourteenth Dalai Lama was forced to flee after the invasion of his country by China.

The invasion led to massive destruction of Buddhist institutions and loss of life. When the Chinese Army arrived, there were more than 7000 Buddhist monasteries, temples and other structures in Tibet. By the end of the Cultural Revolution (1966–76), about only seven were mostly undamaged. Hundreds of thousands of monks and nuns were forced to return to lay life and the contents of monasteries were pillaged. Statues were sold on international markets or melted down for their metal content, whole libraries with irreplaceable collections were ransacked and their books burned and the Tibetan people were forced onto communes. Estimates of Tibetan deaths range from several hundred thousand to more than one million.

After his escape into exile in India in 1959, the fourteenth Dalai Lama, Tenzin Gyatso (1935–) founded a government-in-exile headquartered in Dharamsala, Himachal Pradesh. He was soon joined by tens of thousands of Tibetans who also fled Chinese persecution. Every year, another 3000 make the perilous journey across the world's highest passes to escape religious persecution and human rights abuses in their homeland.

After the harsh repression during the Cultural Revolution, there was a period of relative liberalisation in the 1980s, which ended when large-scale demonstrations erupted across the Tibetan Plateau. This led to a massive and brutal clampdown by Chinese authorities and declaration of martial law in 1989.

Since that time, the official Chinese attitude towards religion has hardened and the government continues to suppress even the slightest dissent with overwhelming force. In March and April 2008, unprecedented numbers of Tibetans took to the streets to air a range of grievances, including economic marginalisation and religious repression. In response, Chinese authorities evicted all tourists and journalists from the region and moved in tens of thousands of heavily armed combat troops. Despite a media blackout, reports emerged of severe repression, widespread use of arbitrary detention and torture. The situation in Tibet remains extremely tense and Chinese authorities show no signs of engaging in meaningful dialogue or of any willingness to relax their repression of the Tibetan population.

Buddhist practice in Tibet is severely restricted by the authorities, but it continues to thrive in exile. In addition, hundreds of thousands of non-Tibetans around the world have converted, and Tibetan masters such as the Dalai Lama often attract huge crowds for their public teachings. In 1989, the Dalai Lama was awarded the Nobel Peace Prize, and in 2008 was given the Congressional Medal of Honor, the highest civilian award in the United States. He is widely regarded as an ambassador for peace and is among the most revered religious leaders in the world. His participation in this conference is an example of his efforts to foster dialogue between religions and his belief that religion properly understood and practised is one of the greatest resources for fostering peace and understanding between individuals and nations.

10. Introduction to Judaism
RABBI PAUL JACOBSEN[1]

The task of introducing the basic tenets and spiritual practices of the Jewish people represents an enormous challenge. First, authors of encyclopaedic volumes fill page after page on the subject of Jewish life and history. These tomes address the triumphs and travails of Jewish civilisation, often seeking to cover more than 3000 years of history in succinct fashion. Second, although the Jewish people have, in the past century, reclaimed Israel as their physical and spiritual homeland, we are and will continue to exist as a scattered multitude living amid people of other cultures and faiths. Third, Jews express their commitment and ideology in diverse ways through a variety of recognised movements and practices. To quote a popular bumper sticker in Israel, 'There is more than one way to be Jewish'.

While each Jew, formulating his or her own opinion in accordance with the ideas and values of our tradition, might offer different perspectives in an essay such as this one, it is still worth exploring the foundational values on which our heritage rests. For all of the division and distance between us, for all of the variety present in Jewish life, there are many practices and principles that unify us as a people. Judaism continues to inform and influence our lives, even today.

The Torah: early history

The Torah (which includes the books of Genesis, Exodus, Leviticus, Numbers and Deuteronomy) presents the earliest history of the Jewish people and the Israelite nation. In the twelfth chapter of Genesis, God selects Abram to participate in a life-changing mission. God says, 'Go forth from your native land and from your father's house to the land that I will show you. I will make of you a great nation, and I will bless you; I will make your name great, and you shall be a blessing.'[2] Abram follows God's command, leaves his birthplace and sets out for unknown horizons. Subsequently, God establishes a special relationship with Abram, known as a covenant—a binding contract between partners.

---

1 Rabbi Paul J. Jacobson earned his rabbinical ordination from Hebrew Union College's Jewish Institute of Religion in Cincinnati, Ohio, in the United States. He currently serves Emanuel Synagogue in Sydney, New South Wales, Australia.
2 Genesis 12:1–2. All biblical translations are taken from *Tanakh: The holy scriptures*, 1988, Jewish Publication Society translation.

In exchange for promising to observe God's commandments, Abram, now known as Abraham, is informed that he will become 'the father of a multitude of nations' and that the land of Canaan (later Israel) will be given to his offspring as an everlasting holding.[3] Furthermore, Abraham's descendants will be enslaved in a foreign nation for more than 400 years, at which time God promises to deliver them into freedom.[4]

Throughout the remainder of Genesis, Israelite history appears as a series of isolated family narratives. Abraham passes the covenant onto his son Isaac, who in turn passes these teachings and responsibilities onto Jacob to uphold.

Only in the generation of Joseph does the story of the Jewish people and the Israelite nation begin to emerge. Sold into slavery by his brothers, Joseph descends into Egypt, where a combination of faith and good fortune allows him to emerge as second-in-command to the Pharaoh. There is a terrible famine in the land of Canaan and Joseph's brothers, unaware of their brother's rise to power and prominence, travel to Egypt in search of food. After a series of encounters, Joseph and his brothers are reunited and Joseph informs his brothers, 'God has sent me ahead of you to ensure your survival on earth, and to save your lives in an extraordinary deliverance.'[5] Joseph's family settles in the land of Egypt and lives there peacefully, under Egyptian rule, for a number of generations.

As time passes, the Israelites grow in number and the leadership of Egypt changes hands. A ruthless Pharaoh takes the throne, enslaving the Israelites and forcing them to labour with bitterness.[6] Pharaoh issues a dreadful command: all Hebrew boys that are born shall be cast into the River Nile, while all Hebrew girls shall be allowed to live.[7]

Moses's story, however, is different. Placed into a wicker basket only three months after his birth, baby Moses drifts down the Nile to where Pharaoh's daughter is bathing. Assuming the child to be of Hebrew descent, Pharaoh's daughter takes the child into her care and raises him in the Pharaoh's palace. As Moses matures, he becomes increasingly aware of the plight of the Hebrew slaves. After Moses kills an Egyptian taskmaster for beating a slave, Pharaoh is incensed, and Moses flees for his life into the wilderness.[8]

In the wilderness, Moses is given an awesome responsibility. One day, while tending the flock of his father-in-law, Jethro,[9] Moses comes across a burning

---

3   Genesis 17:3–8.
4   Genesis 15:13–14.
5   Genesis 45:7.
6   Exodus 1:8–14.
7   Exodus 1:22.
8   Exodus 2:1–15.
9   Exodus 2:16–23. Jethro is referred to here as Reuel. By this time in the narrative, Moses has married Jethro's daughter, Zipporah.

bush that, strangely, is not consumed by the blaze.[10] God speaks to Moses from the bush, acknowledges the difficulties that the Israelites have encountered as slaves in Egypt and promises to rescue them and bring them into the land of Israel.[11] Along with the assistance of his older brother, Aaron, Moses is instructed to approach Pharaoh and request that Pharaoh allow the Israelites to depart the land of Egypt immediately.[12]

Pharaoh's response to Moses and Aaron's request causes the tension of an already untenable situation to escalate even further. Recognising Pharaoh's reluctance to allow the Israelites to flee, God sends a series of plagues against the Egyptian populace. The plagues wreak havoc on the people and the land of Egypt and are perceived as miracles by the Israelite slaves. After 10 dreadful plagues, Pharaoh finally relents and permits the Israelites to depart.[13]

The ultimate redemption of the Israelites, however, is still to come. After marching into the wilderness, freed from slavery, the Israelites find themselves at the shore of the Sea of Reeds. Pharaoh, angered at his decision to release the Israelites, has sent his army in pursuit. The Israelites are trapped. Turning towards the water, Moses implores God for a solution. God commands Moses to lift his rod over the waters and split the sea, so that the Israelites can cross through, miraculously on dry land. With the Egyptian army on their heels, the Israelites cross over to the other side, the waters close once again and the Egyptians are drowned in the sea. The redemption of the Israelites is borne in a moment of suffering and pain for their oppressors.[14]

Having crossed through the sea in a miraculous turn of events, the Israelites are led through the wilderness and encamp at the foot of Mount Sinai. Until now, God has established a relationship with particular individuals. At Sinai, however, God forges bonds with the whole of the Israelite nation. Moses ascends the mountain to receive God's Law, and in a dramatic display with thunder and lightning, the Israelites witness this monumental act of revelation.[15] The Israelites are commanded to abide by all of God's teachings.

From this moment of revelation, the Torah includes not only narratives but laws and commandments. The Israelites contribute to the construction of a tabernacle, a temporary sanctuary in the wilderness, where rituals are observed during their travels.[16]

---

10 Exodus 3:1–3.
11 Exodus 3:4–9.
12 Exodus 4:14–17.
13 Exodus 7–12.
14 Exodus 14–16.
15 Exodus 19–20.
16 See Exodus 35–40 for further detail.

A system for sacrificial worship (arguably, the practice by which many ancient cults pleased their gods) is established in great detail,[17] along with commands for just and ethical behaviour.[18] The Israelites are instructed that they must strive continually to achieve holiness in their lives.[19]

The Israelites struggle, however, with the concept of holiness. Much of the book of Numbers is dedicated to scenes of one rebellion after another. Moses persuades an enraged God to withhold anger and punishment, reminding God of the effort involved in bringing forth the Israelites from the land of Egypt.[20] As Moses continues to tire under the weighty responsibilities of leadership, the Israelites ready for battle; their conquest of the 'Promised Land' draws closer.[21]

Nevertheless, the conquest of Israel does not appear in the Torah. The book of Deuteronomy, the final book of the Torah, serves to retell many events of the Israelites' wanderings, while introducing some new episodes. Deuteronomy also presents more commandments, introducing, among other things, systems for justice and lawful behaviour. At the conclusion of the book, Moses entrusts Joshua with the leadership of the Israelites. As Moses is fated to die, unable to lead the Israelites into the land of Israel, Joshua will need to guide them in their conquest.

The remainder of the Tanakh: later history

While presenting the earliest accounts of Israelite history, the Torah represents only the beginning of the Jewish journey. The Torah is the first of three sections found in the Tanakh, the Hebrew Bible. The word *'tanakh'* is an acronym standing for Torah, *'nevi'im'* (prophets) and *'kethuvim'* (writings). The Tanakh is a composite work. Some texts are historical accounts based on the annals of the early kingdoms; other texts include prophetic visions of impending doom and subsequent redemption; other texts reflect the joys and sorrows of life; and still other texts weave beautiful love poetry into the pages of the Bible.

The historical content found in the first six books of Nevi'im (Joshua, Judges, First and Second Samuel, First and Second Kings) reflects the internal and external tensions experienced by the newly formed Israelite nation. Having successfully conquered the land, the Israelites must confront continuing challenges with

---

17 See Leviticus for further detail.
18 See Leviticus 19 for further detail.
19 Leviticus 19:2.
20 Numbers 14:13–19.
21 See Numbers 27–36 for further detail.

leadership. Although the Israelites decided to appoint a king to rule over them, and many of the kings expanded their territory, it was clear that ancient Jewish civilisation experienced more than its fair share of war and trauma.

By the conclusion of Nevi'im, the Israelites are in disarray as the Babylonian Army, led by Nebuchadnezzar, advances on them and destroys the temple in Jerusalem (586 BCE). Many of the Israelites spend much of the next 70 years in exile or rebuilding Jerusalem.

While the temple in Jerusalem is rebuilt (515 BCE),[22] much of Jewish history and literature enters a dark period. Though the biblical text is canonised during this time, and some information is known about the Maccabean revolt against the Syrians (ca 165 BCE),[23] Jews continue to face confrontations from surrounding countries. Over time, Jews in Israel were subjected to the rule of the Roman Empire, and in 70 CE, the Second Temple in Jerusalem was destroyed.

From biblical to rabbinical times

The destruction of the Second Temple marked a watershed shift in Jewish life. For many generations, the First Temple, and subsequently the Second Temple, stood as the central location for Jewish worship and Jewish life. With the temple destroyed and no opportunity to rebuild under Roman rule, the great dispersion (Diaspora) of the Jewish people began, and Jews began living in various corners of the world.

Yet while there was no opportunity to rebuild the temple, Jews retained the hope that they would be miraculously redeemed, that they would return to the land of Israel and would restore their temple to its glory. In the absence of sacrificial practice, rabbis (teachers of Judaism) sought methods by which they might retain the beauty of Jewish tradition, while helping their people to adapt to new and somewhat untenable circumstances. In the third century CE, Rabbi Judah Ha-Nasi compiled the *Mishnah*, a collection of Jewish laws attempting to preserve ancient practice, while introducing new customs and interpretations.[24]

---

22 This event is recorded in the books of Ezra and Nehemiah, in the third section of the *Tanakh* (Kethuvim). The books of Ezra and Nehemiah are widely accepted by scholars as the latest texts to find their way into the Hebrew Bible.
23 The *Apocrypha* is a collection of works not canonised in the Hebrew Bible. The books of Maccabees, specifically First and Second Maccabees, record the events of this uprising about 165 BCE.
24 The origin of the *Mishnah* represents a point of division for some Jews. Strictly Orthodox Jews regard the Torah as 'Torah *she-bichtav*' (the 'Written Torah') and *Mishnah* and subsequent rabbinical texts as 'Torah *she-baal-peh*' ('Oral Torah'). The Written and Oral Torah for orthodox Jews are considered to have been authored by God and delivered to Moses at the time of revelation on Mount Sinai. Non-fundamentalist Jews recognise the possibility of divine inspiration within revelation and also accept the potential for human influence in our most sacred writings and teachings. Thus, some texts, in contemporary movements, might be regarded by constituents as having been penned by human hands.

In each generation, new rabbis emerged, studying and evaluating the texts and interpretations of their teachers before them. The *Tosefta* supplemented the *Mishnah*, the *Talmud* (a version in Palestine and a version in Babylon) superseded the *Tosefta* and later sages continued to comment on the *Talmud*. Although each generation has added new ideas to those of preceding generations, the *Mishnah*, *Tosefta*, *Talmud* and their accompanying commentaries are still studied in Jewish communities throughout the world in the hope that passages from these extraordinary resources might illuminate contemporary Jewish life even further.

By the Middle Ages, however, the process of Jewish interpretation had become somewhat unwieldy. Because works such as the *Talmud* were written as a series of lengthy conversations between rabbis about various issues, it became difficult for the lay Jew to discern the proper manner of Jewish observance. To be fair, rabbis had always been involved in the process of creating *halakhah*,[25] the pathway of Jewish law and life, but the end result of their conversations was not always as readily accessible as it could have been. Maimonides, among other sages, sought to create texts, such as the *Mishneh Torah*, which simplified the discussions found in earlier rabbinical works, helping the average Jew to understand his heritage and faith. Such a process continued throughout subsequent generations with works such as the *Shulkhan Arukh*[26] and in recent centuries the *Mishnah Berurah*.[27] It is important to note that each generation of Jewish law builds on the writings and teachings of the generations before it.

Divisions within contemporary Jewish life

The *halakhic* process continues in Judaism today but with widely different implications for Jews of different communities and backgrounds. Since the early nineteenth century, noticeable schisms have been present in Jewish communal life. The 'Reform' movement arose in Europe and later planted itself firmly in the fabric of American Jewish culture as a response to the ancient, unfamiliar practices of Orthodoxy. Those involved in the process of reform sought to change Judaism, to enable it to adapt to the contemporary needs of its constituents, bringing egalitarianism and the language of the vernacular into prayer and study. There were, however, those among the Jewish community

---

25 The word 'halakhah' originates from the Hebrew verb meaning 'to go'. Thus, *halakhah* can be rendered as 'the path upon which one goes/travels'. Although *halakhah* often refers to Jewish law, it is also regarded as the pathway of Jewish life, including the practices by which a traditional Jew will abide.
26 Written in the sixteenth century by Joseph Karo, the work translates as 'The Set Table'.
27 A late nineteenth–early twentieth-century work edited by the Chofetz Chayim.

who, recognising the need for change, believed that the Reform movement had gone too far, ignoring basic foundational customs such as the Sabbath and dietary observance (*kashrut*).[28]

In an effort to toe a tenuous line between the strictures of Orthodoxy and the liberalism of Reform, a Conservative movement was forged, seeking to preserve and respect the *halakhic* process, while incorporating the need for change and contemporary development.[29]

Each of the three major movements within Jewish life presents different ideologies. For most observant Orthodox Jews, the Torah and subsequent generations of rabbinical interpretation are God given. The origin of Jewish tradition is God and God is served by a connection to commandments and Jewish community. For most Conservative and Reform Jews, however, questions of ideology and practice are not defined as easily. Conservative Jews tend to acknowledge the importance of revelation as a singularly defining event in Jewish history, an establishment of the relationship between God and the Jewish people.

The process by which the Torah is infused into Jewish life requires, however, human interpretation and human assistance. While some Reform Jews would acknowledge revelation with great significance, members of the Reform movement as a whole appear more willing to recognise the divinely inspired nature of religious text and the presence of the human hand in textual development. By no means are we asserting that God is absent from Jewish life in the Reform world, only that Reform Jews establish their relationship with God, and discover God's presence, in ways not limited to God as 'Author' or 'Commander' of the traditions.[30]

Naturally though, the ideologies of each movement have had great influence on the level of practice observed within each movement. One is more likely to discover greater ritual observance and familiarity with tradition within Orthodox and Conservative communities than in Reform communities.[31] To their benefit, members of the Reform Jewish world have begun, in the past 20 or so years, to explore greater connection to traditional practice. Even though the early reformers disregarded traditional ideas such as the observance of the Sabbath, dietary laws and connection to the land of Israel, twenty-first-century

---

28 These ideas will be explored below.
29 There are other movements within Jewish life as well. In the interest of space, however, I list only the three movements that have the greatest number of followers today.
30 It is important to note that 'Reform' tends to be a term used to explain 'liberal Jewish life' in the United States. The term generally used throughout the world is 'Progressive'. Similarly, 'Conservative Judaism' is a term found most commonly in the United States. The term generally used throughout the world is the Hebrew equivalent, 'Masorti' ('traditional').
31 This is not to say that one will not find unobservant Orthodox or Conservative Jews, only that the percentage of religiously observant Jews is higher in the Orthodox world than in the Conservative or Reform Jewish world.

Reform Jews are busy reclaiming these practices and beliefs as their own, establishing strong bonds with the State of Israel and unearthing new ways to appreciate these important Jewish precepts.

A moment of transition: from history to practice

In the first part of this essay, we endeavoured to provide a basic historical overview of Jewish life and Jewish text. Undoubtedly, readers will, at some point or another, have heard the Jewish people referred to by the term 'People of the Book'. Truly, we are, and continue to be, a 'people of many books'. In order to provide even an elementary understanding of our basic spiritual practices, we first need to acknowledge the texts and process by which these spiritual practices came to emerge. Without an explanation of the various books that make up our tradition, and recognition of the continuing intellectual pursuit involved in Jewish life, any explanation of customs is simply incomplete. And even though there are divisions and a multiplicity of observances found throughout the world, there are still a number of practices that unify us as a people, which we will attempt to explore below.

God and the Covenant

Jews share a belief in one and only one God. Though each Jew may have a different way of connecting with or expressing their belief in God, a common current that runs through Jewish life is the affirmation of the oneness, the indivisibility of God. Jews are commanded to recite the words of the *Sh'ma* twice daily,[32] thereby acknowledging God's presence in the universe and rekindling a commitment to uphold the practices of Jewish life.

God appears in many ways throughout biblical and rabbinical tradition. God creates the universe, reveals Jewish law to the people and redeems the Israelites from their enslavement, leading them to the land of Israel. In some texts, God is seen as a judge, who metes out punishment and chastisement. In other texts, God is compassionate and merciful, showing the Jewish people forgiveness and continuing love and allowing Jews to return in repentance. In many ways, both the 'judging' and 'compassionate' side are necessary. We need to live a Jewish life grounded in structure, appreciating and performing the laws developed throughout the generations and we also need the presence of a loving, kind God who will support us, enable us to do our best and give us the strength and courage to carry on.

---

[32] Deuteronomy 6:4: 'Hear O Israel, the LORD is our God, the LORD is One.'

As explained earlier in this essay, God established a relationship with Abraham known as a covenant—a special bond between two parties. Consequently, each Jew is personally involved in a covenantal relationship with God.

As God promised, many generations ago, to offer Abraham and his descendants life, blessings, prosperity and land, so too do we uphold our covenant with God through our observance of *mitzvot*. *Mitzvot* (singular: *mitzvah*) are commandments including those relating to ethical behaviour, festival observances and other practices that a Jew is obliged to keep (explored in greater detail below). Contrary to popular belief, a *mitzvah* is not just a good deed; it is a duty commanded for a Jew to observe and practise.

Interestingly enough, there is no command anywhere in Jewish tradition 'to believe in God'. Rather, a Jewish person is obligated to 'love God with all of your heart, all of your soul, and all of your being'.[33] Jews discover and appreciate, wrestle with and question God's presence in many different ways. We find God, among other places, in the awesomeness of nature, in the intimacy of our relationships and throughout the vicissitudes of our most personal experiences. Just as our ancestors sensed God's presence embracing them during times of joy and turned to God in moments of sorrow, so too do we turn to God, publicly and privately, through communal expression and through the words of our own hearts. By showing our love, our respect and appreciation for the world and people around us, we demonstrate our love for God.

The synagogue: prayers and the reading of the Torah

Traditionally, observant Jews pray three times a day: in the evening, morning and afternoon. The times of prayer correspond with the times when sacrifice was offered in the ancient temple in Jerusalem. While it is possible for a Jew to pray any time in any place, Jewish life affirms the notion of communal prayer. In Jewish experience, formal prayer requires the presence of 10 Jewish adults, a quorum known in Hebrew as *minyan*. In Orthodox Jewish law, only males over the age of thirteen may constitute a *minyan*. Similarly, men and women sit separately from one another in an orthodox synagogue and only men participate in the worship service. In accordance with egalitarianism, Conservative and Reform Jews will include women in a quorum for prayers and allow women to participate in the leadership of prayers.

---

33 Deuteronomy 6:5.

Although services may happen anywhere that Jews gather and are knowledgeable enough to recite the liturgy, synagogues are often regarded as proper Jewish houses of worship. A synagogue fulfils three functions: it is at once a *beit Knesset*, a communal house of gathering; a *beit t'filah*, a house of prayer; and a *beit midrash*, a house of learning.

Given the number of tragedies that have befallen the Jewish people throughout history, many Jews often express a more agnostic approach to prayer and theology. A common question often found in Jewish circles is, 'Where was God during the Holocaust?' While many theologians and philosophers have attempted to address the problems of evil in the world, to answer questions of theodicy and to explain 'why bad things happen to good people', such questions, we find, have very few, if any, satisfactory answers.

The purpose of prayer is not necessarily to find answers to difficult questions, but to provide community, support and time for condolence and reflection. Even when we are bowed with sorrow or face difficult circumstances, prayer affords us an opportunity to connect with God, to express our deepest emotions and to affirm what is good, decent and beautiful about our lives.

Formal prayer services are conducted out of a book called a *siddur* (the collected order of Jewish prayers) and prayers include psalms, biblical passages and other writings praising God and showing appreciation for God's role as Creator, Revealer and Redeemer. A section of each service is dedicated to personal prayers and supplications, for our rabbis teach that if we do not take the effort to personalise our prayers, it is as if we have not fulfilled our duty to pray.

On the Sabbath and festive days, the liturgy is longer, and in many congregations, the services include joyful, participatory singing. While traditionally observant Jews will abstain from using musical instruments during their service,[34] Reform and Conservative Jews are more open to this practice.

Over the course of many generations, rabbis developed a calendar for the reading of the Torah, thereby dividing the five books of the Torah into 54 weekly sections.[35] A portion of the Torah is read on the Sabbath each week. On festivals, a reading related to the theme of that particular day or season is read.[36] Additionally, a selection from the words of the prophets, known as *haftarah*, is chanted.[37] Similar to their approach to the leadership of prayer, Orthodox Jews

---

34 Orthodox Jews hold the belief that until the temple in Jerusalem is restored to its glory, music should not accompany prayer services.
35 Some Conservative communities retain the practice of reading the entire Torah once every three years. In most Reform communities, only a small section of the Torah is read every week.
36 The Torah is traditionally read, in addition to Sabbath morning and festive occasions, on Monday and Thursday mornings, Sabbath afternoons and on fast days.
37 The word 'haftarah' means 'conclusion' because it is the final reading in the section of the service when the Torah is read aloud. *Haftarah* is often read from a book, not usually from a scroll like the Torah.

allow only men to be called to the Torah for the honour of reciting blessings over the scroll, to read from the Torah or to read the *haftarah*. Conservative and Reform Jews invite women to participate in each aspect of synagogue ritual.

Learning, life cycle and good deeds

There is more to Jewish life than prayer. A passage from the *Talmud*, traditionally recited each morning during prayer, summarises Jewish obligations beautifully:

> These are the commandments which yield immediate fruit and continue to yield fruit in time to come: honouring parents, doing deeds of loving kindness, attending the house of study punctually, morning and evening, providing hospitality, visiting the sick, helping the needy bride, attending the dead, devotion in prayer, and making peace between people. And the study of Torah is basic to them all.[38]

Even though many Jews hold the belief that the 'Ten Commandments'[39] are a central part of Jewish life, the commandments included in that section of the Torah are basic observances, the fulfilment of which applies to many cultures and civilisations throughout the world. In contrast, the above text from the Babylonian *Talmud* summarises basic *Jewish* obligations, including participation in prayer and life-cycle events, the study of the Torah and ethical behaviour.

Such concepts and duties are echoed throughout life-cycle ceremonies. In Jewish tradition, baby boys are circumcised when they are eight days old. The circumcision ceremony is more than a mere cutting of flesh; through this ancient rite, the child is welcomed into the covenant of the Jewish people. Those present at such a ceremony express the hope that just as this child has entered into the covenant, so too may he achieve a life dedicated to the learning of the Torah, one day celebrate his marriage under the *chuppah* (the Jewish wedding canopy) and always perform *ma'asim tovim* (good deeds). Similarly, baby girls may be welcomed into the community and the covenant of the Jewish people through a naming ceremony.

As children grow older, they are reared in the ways of their tradition. Although synagogues are regarded as central locations for prayer and study, Jewish life begins at home. Parents need to model appropriate Jewish behaviour, teaching Judaism to their children, creating a home in which Jewish values are modelled and where the Sabbath and festivals are celebrated.[40]

---

38   *Babylonian Talmud* Shabbat 127a. Translation taken from Harlow, J. (ed.) *1978, Mahzor for Rosh Hashanah and Yom Kippur: A prayer book for the days of* awe, The Rabbinical Assembly, New York, p. 67.
39   See Exodus 20 or Deuteronomy 5 for further details.
40   Deuteronomy 6:7.

At the age of twelve, girls become *Bat Mitzvah*[41] and at the age of thirteen boys become *Bar Mitzvah*. The term '*Bar/Bat Mitzvah*' translates as 'one legally bound by the commandments'. Until this point, parents have been responsible for the child's Jewish upbringing.

Now, as a child begins to mature, s/he is capable of accepting additional Jewish responsibilities and is regarded as having adult status in the Jewish community. *Bar/Bat Mitzvah* is often celebrated in the synagogue. In Orthodox communities, boys are called to recite blessings over the Torah scroll and participate in the religious service, while girls celebrate communally or by offering a small speech about a passage of the Torah. In Conservative and Reform communities, boys and girls participate in the religious service.

The hope for any Jewish child is that s/he will fall in love, marry a Jewish partner and establish a Jewish home. Judaism places significant emphasis on the importance of marriage and respects the intimacy shared by husband and wife. In the context of marriage, husband and wife are instructed to have children of their own, accepting their responsibility as teachers and inculcators of Jewish practices and values.

In addition to the celebration of various life-cycle occasions, however, there are basic customs associated with Jewish life and observance. In all respects, we are supposed to copy the best of God's behaviours; we are to be holy, because God is considered to be holy.[42] Holiness extends throughout a variety of ethical practices. As Jews, we must attend to the needs of others compassionately, concern ourselves with the wellbeing of animals and the environment and care for the stranger, because we were strangers, long ago, in the land of Egypt.

Holiness is present in our dietary obligations too. The Torah and subsequent generations of rabbinical literature established a disciplinary system from which we would become more conscious of the food we ate. Traditionally, observant Jews will abstain from certain foods.[43] The animals eaten must both chew their cud and have cloven hoofs, and fish must have fins and scales. Animals need to be slaughtered in the most humane way possible, reducing their suffering. Items containing meat and milk are not consumed in the same meal.

Jews also participate in acts of social justice, often by volunteering their time and/or money to a variety of charities and supporting a number of communal causes. Deuteronomy commands us: 'Justice, justice, you shall pursue.'[44] At the conclusion of every prayer service, we read the words '*L'taken olam b'malchut*

---

41 In some communities, girls celebrate becoming *bat mitzvah* at the age of thirteen.
42 Leviticus 19:2.
43 See Leviticus 11 and Deuteronomy 14 for further details.
44 Deuteronomy 16:20.

Shaddai', reminding us that Jews must perfect the world under the sovereignty of God. Even as we dedicate ourselves to the mission of *tikkun olam*—the repair of the world—we recognise that there is much to do before the world is fully redeemed. We also know that we need to work together with people of other faiths and practices to help achieve a peaceful, sustainable vision for the future of our world.

Living in Jewish time

The origin of *Shabbat*, the Jewish Sabbath, is recorded in the opening chapters of the Torah. According to the biblical tradition, God created the world in six days and then rested and was refreshed on the seventh day.[45] *Shabbat* reminds us not only of the events of creation but of our ancestors' redemption from slavery. In a historical sense, *Shabbat* marked the time in which everyone, including men, women, slaves and animals, were freed from their labours and given an opportunity to celebrate and reflect.

The Sabbath is observed from sunset on Friday evening until approximately one hour after sunset on Saturday night and is known in Hebrew as *Shabbat*. In accordance with historical norms and commandments, traditionally observant Jews cease all labour on *Shabbat*. *Shabbat* is a time to pray, sing, to eat celebratory meals, learn, rest and socialise with family and friends.

It is also worth noting that *Shabbat* is considered central to a Jew's week. In Hebrew, Sunday is known as *yom rishon* (the first day of the week), Monday is known as *yom sheni* (the second day of the week), and so on. With each day, a Jew knows how many days have elapsed since *Shabbat* and how many days it will be until *Shabbat* arrives again. As twentieth-century theologian Abraham Joshua Heschel has taught, *Shabbat* affords us the opportunity to experience 'holiness in time'.[46]

Observant Jews make every effort to live in Jewish time. In Jewish tradition, the calendar is lunar based on a 354-day year. Additionally, the calendar is solar adjusted. Since a number of our festivals have agricultural origins, it is necessary to make alterations to our calendar so that festivals will be observed in the proper season. Approximately once every three years, within a 19-year cycle, an additional month is added to the Jewish calendar, helping to offset the differences that occur in the lunar calendar.[47]

---

45   See Genesis 1:1–2:3 for further detail.
46   Heschel, A. J. 1983, *God in Search of Man: A philosophy of Judaism*, Farrar, Straus and Giroux, New York, p. 417.
47   For example, this year (2009), the festival of *Rosh Hashanah* (Jewish New Year) occurs on 19 September. Next year (2010), *Rosh Hashanah* will fall on 9 September. In 2011, however—a leap year in the calendar—

Jews celebrate a number of festivals throughout the year. The Torah records, in addition to *Shabbat*, the origin of five major festival observances still practised today, including *Pesach* (Passover: the Feast of Unleavened Bread), *Shavuot* (Feast of First Fruits/Weeks), *Rosh Hashanah* (Jewish New Year), *Yom Kippur* (Day of Atonement) and *Sukkot* (Feast of Booths/Ingathering).

In the first month of the calendar,[48] Jews observe *Pesach*.[49] *Pesach* commemorates the exodus from Egypt. Jews participate in a special meal known as a *seder* and read from a text known as the *Haggadah*, a rabbinical discourse on the concepts of the exodus. The *seder* table includes many symbolic items: bitter herbs,[50] salt water,[51] a lamb shank bone,[52] a roasted egg[53] and a green vegetable.[54] Additionally, because the Israelites' bread did not have time to rise when they departed Egypt, Jews eat *matzah* (unleavened bread) during *Pesach* and abstain from eating products with any kind of leavening agents.

Seven weeks after *Pesach*, Jews celebrate *Shavuot*. In ancient times, *Shavuot* held greater significance as an agricultural festival than it does today. *Shavuot* was regarded as the Festival of the First Fruits and the first offerings of the harvest were brought to the ancient Temple in Jerusalem. Over time, *Shavuot* acquired new meaning. Based on the dating of the stories found in the Torah, our rabbis reckoned that *Shavuot* also marked the time of the revelation of the Torah. It is customary to decorate the synagogue with fruit and greenery and also to spend the entire night of *Shavuot* engaged in study, thus acknowledging both aspects of this festive celebration.

The seventh month of the calendar[55]—arguably the conclusion of the agricultural season in the land of Israel—brought further commemorations and celebrations. The Torah teaches that on the first day of the seventh month, 'a sacred occasion commemorated with loud blasts' was observed.[56] This biblical verse has become the origin of the festival of *Rosh Hashanah*, the Jewish New Year. On *Rosh Hashanah*, Jews celebrate the creation of the world and acclaim the sovereignty

---

Rosh Hashanah will fall on 29 September. A leap year helps maintain the festivals in the appropriate season, even if, each year, the date will vary slightly in the secular calendar.
48 Anytime between the end of March and mid April.
49 In Israel and in many Reform communities, *Pesach* is celebrated for seven days. In traditionally observant communities outside Israel, *Pesach* is observed for eight days.
50 Symbolising the bitterness of slavery.
51 Symbolising tears.
52 Symbolising the *Pesach* sacrifice. Additionally, the night before the Israelites' departure from slavery in Egypt, the tenth plague occurred and God killed all Egyptian first-born sons. To identify which houses were Israelite houses, and to therefore shield families from this plague, Israelites slaughtered a lamb and painted blood on the doorpost of their house. God therefore 'passed over' their houses, saving their sons.
53 Symbolising the cyclical nature of life and the additional sacrifice offered in the temple in ancient times on Pesach.
54 Symbolising springtime and serving as an entrée for the meal.
55 Anytime between early September and early October.
56 Leviticus 23:25.

of God. Further, the *shofar*, a ram's horn, is sounded during services, calling us into a period of repentance and introspection, as it is said that God judges our existence during this time. This 10-day period concludes with *Yom Kippur*, the Day of Atonement, on which Jews spend the day in a synagogue, praying and fasting, making attempts to repair their relationship with God and with friends and family.

Shortly after *Yom Kippur*, on the fifteenth day of the seventh month, Jews observe *Sukkot* for seven days. When the Israelites were wandering in the wilderness, they dwelt in booths—temporary shelters—and we reclaim this practice by eating celebratory meals (and sometimes sleeping) in similarly fragile structures. Jews also have the custom of waving the *lulav* (a combination of palm, myrtle and willow branches) and *etrog* (a citron-like fruit) together, to acknowledge God's omnipresence.

Because *Sukkot* falls at the conclusion of the agricultural calendar, and Jews spend so much time outdoors, formal prayers for rain are not included in the service until the day of *Shemini Atzeret*, the twenty-second day of the seventh month. The next day, Jews celebrate *Simchat Torah*, a joyful festival in which community members dance with the Torah scrolls, conclude the reading of the book of Deuteronomy and begin the reading of the Torah from Genesis once again.

In addition to the festivals mentioned in the Torah, the rabbis instituted a number of important commemorations. *Tu B'Shevat*[57] celebrates the birthday of trees. *Purim*[58] affords Jews an opportunity for merrymaking in the synagogue as we read from the book of Esther and recall her valiant efforts to successfully thwart the king's adviser, Haman, in his effort to destroy the Jews of Persia. *Tisha B'Av*[59] is a mournful day on which we commemorate the destruction of the ancient temples in Jerusalem and other tragedies that have befallen the Jewish people in history. *Chanukah*[60] celebrates the victory of the Maccabees over the Syrians in 165 BCE and the subsequent rededication of the temple. In more contemporary times, we also observe *Yom Ha-Shoah* (Holocaust Remembrance Day), *Yom Ha-Zikaron* (Memorial Day for Israeli Soldiers and Victims of Terrorism), *Yom Ha-Atzmaut* (Israel's Day of Independence) and *Yom Yerushalayim* (Jerusalem Day).

---

57 Usually falls in late January or early February.
58 Usually falls in late February to mid March.
59 Usually falls in mid July to late August.
60 Usually falls some time during December.

Commitment to Israel

Jews have always recognised Israel as their physical and spiritual homeland. Traditionally minded Jews regard the land as having been promised by God to Abraham in ancient times. The Hebrew Bible records that our biblical ancestors conquered the land and established systems for leadership, justice and worship. Further, most of the events described in the Hebrew Bible occurred in the land of Israel.

Yet while the Israelites, and later the Jewish people, inhabited the land for more than a millennium, they spent nearly 2000 years longing to get back. The destruction of the First and Second Temples in Jerusalem, nearly 600 years apart, marked watershed moments in the history of Jewish life and culture.

Israel accepted a central place in Jewish liturgy; prayers in the synagogue and at mealtimes expressed a communal desire to rebuild and resettle the land and to re-establish ancient systems of justice and worship.[61]

Even with the founding of the modern-day State of Israel in 1948, such prayers continue to be offered. The founding of Israel is regarded in Hebrew as '*reishit tz'michat g'ulateinu*', the first flowering of our redemption. Nevertheless, Jews living in Israel and in communities outside Israel are well aware of the attention accorded Israel by the international media. We sincerely hope that Israel will act as a beacon of light and justice, representing what is best about Jewish life and culture to the world. As we dedicate ourselves to Israel's continuing survival in secure borders, we recognise the challenges encountered in the Middle East region and we pray that peaceful solutions will emerge enabling people of different religious and ethnic backgrounds to coexist side by side.

Relationships with people of other faiths

Even as we acknowledge in the preceding section the pursuit of peace, we must not blind ourselves to the fact that the Torah, in addition to providing the history, laws and foundations for Jewish life, is also, at its core, a conquest narrative. Just like many other cultures in world history, the Israelites took possession of the land by force. As the Israelites sought to abolish idol worship and promote monotheism, they were instructed to 'destroy all the sites at which the nations…worshiped their gods…Tear down their altars, smash their pillars, put their sacred posts to the fire, and cut down the images of their gods'.[62] With

---

61   Some Orthodox Jews believe that Israel will be fully established only when God sends the Messiah and brings about the ultimate redemption of the world.
62   Deuteronomy 12:2–3.

such perspectives recorded in the Torah—arguably our people's most revered work—it is difficult to make claims for the importance of inter-faith work and dialogue.

Fortunately, Jewish commitment to inter-faith relations has developed over time.[63] Because Jews became accustomed to living under the dominion of other governments—some more oppressive than others, some more respectful than others—Jews needed to find ways to live amid foreign cultures. Throughout rabbinical literature, inter-faith relations are entered into *'mipnei darchei shalom'*—in the interest of maintaining peace. Jews extend pleasantries with people of other faiths, tend to the needs of those who are ill, may participate in the burial of a non-Jew, will offer charity to non-Jewish organisations and are obliged to treat others (including strangers, orphans and widows) with respect, compassion and decency.

In the present age, when there are so many people who hold such different faith backgrounds, Jews have much to learn not only about their own religion, but about the religions practised by others. The Jewish people have come a long way since the conquest explained in the Torah, and we have more that we can yet accomplish, working together with and learning from each of our neighbours.

Working for ultimate redemption

Throughout this essay, we have addressed Jewish history and Jewish values and we have engendered further conversation on the place of Jews in contemporary society. What, however, is the ultimate goal of being Jewish and living Jewishly? Earlier in this essay, we mentioned the importance of perfecting the world under the sovereignty of God, and it is to this idea that we return at this essay's conclusion. In both beautiful and tragic moments, Jews have retained hope in the coming of a messianic age, a time that will bring redemption, healing and peace to our battered world. We cannot know when God will send the Messiah, but we can make individual and communal efforts to help make such a dream a reality, speeding along the redemptive process. The Reform movement's prayer book, *Gates of Prayer*, offers us words by which to conclude:

> O God, we give thanks for many things, but there is much to do before we can be content with our world. We give thanks for Your creation: for sun and moon, for sea and sky, for bird and beast, for snow and mist, for city streets, for country lanes, for all that lives, for all that makes Your

---

63 It should be noted that by inter-faith relations, the author refers to the work of various faiths to support efforts for coexistence and peace, not to inter-faith relations as one might enter into for the sake of marriage. Different Jewish communities have varied opinions on the subject of intermarriage and assimilation—topics that are beyond the scope of this essay.

children happy. But we remember that there is much to do, before we can be content: the lost and hungry to be found and fed, the sick and the sad to be healed and cheered, a peaceful world to be built and kept, wrongs to be set right, and people to be taught. May we learn, O God, to make this beautiful world a place of goodness and happiness for all Your children.[64]

---

[64] Central Conference of American Rabbis 1975, *Gates of Prayer: The new union prayerbook*, Central Conference of American Rabbis, New York, p. 386.

11. Introduction to Islam
PROFESSOR ABDULLAH SAEED,
UNIVERSITY OF MELBOURNE

Islam

Islam is one of the world's major religions. Today, there are approximately 1.3 billion Muslims in the world. Twenty-two per cent of the world's population is Muslim and 57 countries have Muslim majorities. Although most Muslims live in majority-Muslim countries, approximately one-third live as minorities in countries such as India, China, Russia and France. Twenty million Muslims live in Europe and the Americas.

Although Islam began in Arabia in an Arabic-speaking environment, not all Muslims are Arabs. In fact, only approximately 20 per cent of the world's Muslim population can be considered Arabs. The countries with the largest Muslim populations, except for Egypt, are all outside of the Arab region, including Indonesia, Pakistan, Bangladesh, India, Turkey, Iran and Nigeria.

The advent of Islam

Islam began in the town of Mecca in Arabia (modern-day Saudi Arabia), a commercial town on the trade route between the south and north of Arabia. As well as being a bustling trade centre, Mecca had a rich religious life, fuelled by the beliefs that traders and others brought to the town. The Meccans themselves were pagans and worshipped a large number of idols. Christians and Jews also passed through the town regularly and in some cases some native Meccans converted to these religions. The Meccan people were therefore aware of concepts such as God, prophets and scripture even before the Prophet Muhammad began to teach the religion of Islam.

The Prophet Muhammad

The Prophet Muhammad was born in 570 CE in Mecca. His father, Abd Allah, was a Meccan merchant who died just before Muhammad's birth. Muhammad's mother, Aminah, died when Muhammad was just six years old, leaving him in the care of his grandfather, Abd al-Muttalib, who died just two years later. From then on, Muhammad was brought up by his uncle, Abu Talib.

Muhammad was known in Mecca for his honesty, integrity and hard work. In his early twenties, his reputation brought him to work as a merchant in the caravan trade for a wealthy widowed Meccan businesswoman called Khadijah.

Because of Muhammad's integrity and honesty, Khadijah eventually proposed marriage to him when he was twenty-five years old. Despite their age difference, he accepted. They were married for 25 years until Khadijah died in 619 CE. Together, they had two sons and four daughters.

Muhammad liked to spend time reflecting and meditating away from the busy life of Mecca. When he was in his thirties, he began to spend time alone in a nearby cave called Hira, just outside Mecca. It was there, during one of these times of reflection, that he received his first revelation from God. On this day, while inside the cave, he heard a voice addressing him, asking him to 'read' without saying exactly what to read. The voice asked him to read three times. Each time, Muhammad said, 'I cannot read.' The third time, the voice said: 'Read in the name of your Lord, who created—created Man [human beings] out of a germ-cell. Read—for your Lord is the Most Bountiful One who has taught [man] by the pen—taught Man what he did not know.'[1] This short passage became the first revealed text of the Qur'an.

Muhammad was deeply disturbed by this experience and he returned home in a hurry to Khadijah, who tried to calm and comfort him. After the initial doubts had passed, Muhammad realised that God had given him a mission. He began to preach this message to his family and close friends and relatives. His wife was Islam's first believer, followed by his children and some close relatives and friends.

His teaching began to spread slowly and he had a few converts. They settled in a town in the north called Yathrib, which promised to protect and support the Prophet and his followers. Yathrib, or Medina, became known as the 'City of the Prophet' and there the Muslims established their first community, in 622 CE. Medina became the capital of the first Islamic 'state', and for the next 10 years, the Prophet continued to teach his message there with great success.

When Prophet Muhammad died in 632 CE, the revelations from God ended and the mission of the Prophet was complete. Abu Bakr, the Prophet's close friend and advisor, was nominated to succeed the Prophet as the leader of the Muslims and he became the first political leader or ruler of the community after the Prophet's death.

---

1   Qur'an 96:1–5.

The spread of Islam

The four rulers who managed the affairs of the Muslims after the Prophet's death—Abu Bakr, Umar, Uthman and Ali—are known as the Rashidun caliphs or the 'Rightly Guided' caliphs. Between 632 CE and 661 CE, the Muslim state expanded well beyond the borders of Arabia, to North Africa and to Central Asia.

Under Abu Bakr's rule, various Arab tribes, who had previously accepted Muhammad's authority, rebelled against Abu Bakr and refused to pay *zakat*—their obligatory charitable giving. A series of military campaigns followed, called the 'Ridda Wars' or the 'Wars of Apostasy', which eventually reconsolidated these tribal areas under Abu Bakr's authority.

Shortly after that, Muslims began a series of conquests, directed largely at the Byzantine and Sassanid Empires, located in the north-west and north-east of Arabia, respectively. The Sassanian Empire was brought to an end within a short period and the Byzantines lost most of their possessions in the Middle East and North Africa, bringing these conquered populations under Muslim rule.

The Umayyad Period, from 661 to 750 CE, followed the Rashidun Caliphate. This period in Islam's history was also marked by great territorial expansion. The Muslim state was at its most expansive from 668 to 715 CE, under the leadership of Caliph Abd al-Malik. At this time, it extended from Spain to Central Asia and India, cementing the Umayyad Caliphate's place as one of the largest empires in history.

The Abbasid Period, from 750 to 1258 CE, followed the Umayyad and was also a very significant period of Islamic history. The Abbasid caliphs focused on developing a cohesive community among the Muslim believers. At this time, the Muslim empire was a great melting pot of different cultures, which presented unique opportunities for the Muslim state. Under the Abbasid caliphs, knowledge and innovation were encouraged, drawing from all the different cultures and traditions of the empire. The Abbasids encouraged translation of Greek, Persian and Indian scientific, philosophical and some literary works, and supported scientific research and educational institutions. Scholars functioning within the Muslim caliphate—be they Christians, Jews or Muslims—went on to make significant contributions to various fields, including the arts, agriculture, economics, industry, law, literature, philosophy, the sciences and technology. The time of the Abbasid caliphs came to be known as the 'golden age' of Islamic civilisation.

One World—Many Paths to Peace

Muslim beliefs

The six articles of belief

There are certain beliefs in Islam that are central to the Muslim faith. These are called the six articles of belief or the six pillars of faith, and they function in some ways like the Islamic creed. Despite differences in belief or doctrine among Muslims—for example, between Sunni and Shi'a Muslims—these six essential beliefs are common to all Muslims.

Belief in one God

Muslims frequently refer to God as *Allah*, which means 'the God' in Arabic. The most fundamental belief of a Muslim is that there is no god but God. In Islam, this means there is only one God and there are no other gods besides Him. God was not created; He has always existed and will always exist; He has no beginning or end. When the end of the universe comes, it will be the end of time, but God will remain forever. All other beliefs and practices in Islam are based on this belief in one God.

Muslims believe that God, the Creator and Sustainer, created the universe and everything in it—from galaxies down to microscopic bacteria—and they stand in ultimate testimony to the proof of His existence. When Muslims say that God created the universe, they do not know how it came about or how long it took. The Qur'an says only that the universe was created by God's will and with a single command: 'Be!' For Muslims, there is no contradiction between the possibility that God created the universe in a single instant or through a process of evolution over billions of years.

Muslims also believe that God created human beings at some point. The Qur'an says: 'We created the human being from sounding clay, from mud moulded into shape.'[2]

Within the order of creation, men and women were given a special place by God. Muslims do not believe that humankind was made in God's image; Islam teaches that God breathed his own spirit into humankind, uniquely privileging them over other beings, but not creating them as an image or representation of Himself.

---

2   15:26.

Belief in the prophets and messengers

Another core belief of Muslims is in the prophets and messengers. Part of God's promise to Adam and Eve was that their descendants would be sent prophets who would bring guidance from God. Muslims believe that God sent thousands of prophets to humanity, beginning with Adam, the first prophet, and ending with Muhammad. Many of the prophets mentioned in the Qur'an also feature in the Bible—for example, Abraham, Isaac, Ishmael, Jacob, Noah, Lot and Jesus.

God sent these prophets for a particular purpose—to bring His message to the people of the Earth. The prophets that came before Muhammad were tasked with bringing God's revelation to specific groups or nations of people. Muslims believe that no people were excluded from hearing God's message. Muslims believe that all prophets brought essentially the same message to humankind: that people have a duty to recognise God, the Creator, and to submit to His will. Submission is referred to as *islam* in Arabic—thus, all prophets, from Adam and Abraham to Moses, Jesus and Muhammad, are 'submitters' to God and therefore '*muslims*'.

The Prophet Muhammad has a special place in the Islamic faith. He was the final prophet sent by God and therefore sometimes known as the 'Seal of the Prophets'. When the Prophet Muhammad's name is mentioned, Muslims often use the phrase 'peace be upon him' as a mark of respect.

Belief in the revealed scriptures

Muslims believe that some of the revelations brought by the prophets and messengers who came before Muhammad were written down and preserved as 'revealed books'. Islam recognises the Gospel or *Injil* of Jesus, the Psalms or *Zabur* of David and the Torah or *Tawrat* given to Moses as revealed books. For Muslims, the basic message contained in these scriptures is the same as that of the Qur'an: to believe in God and to live life according to His will.

For Muslims, the final scripture is the Holy Qur'an. The Qur'an is held to be literally the speech of God, not the words or opinions of the Prophet Muhammad or any other human being. For Muslims, the words of the Qur'an today are exactly the same as those revealed to Muhammad, not modern interpretations or applications of the original message. The Qur'an forms the basis of Islamic law, ethics and belief, and is recited by Muslims daily during prayers and at other important moments in life.

Belief in angels

Belief in angels is an important Muslim belief. Although the Qur'an often mentions angels, not much is known about them—what they look like, how many there are or what their functions are. Islamic texts reveal, however, that angels were created from light in order to serve God, and some have specific purposes or functions. Some angels are mentioned by name in the Qur'an. Gabriel (or *Jibril* in Arabic) is the angel who is believed to take revelations or messages from God to His prophets. He is believed to have conveyed the revelations of the Qur'an to the Prophet Muhammad and to have announced to Mary that she would give birth to Jesus.

Belief in the Day of Judgment

Muslims believe there will be a Day of Judgment for all humankind. On this 'day' (whose length is known only to God), every person will be held accountable to God for the actions in their lifetime. God will bring back to life all human beings and gather them together, showing each person everything they have done in this life. Those who lived a 'good' or moral life in line with God's instructions will be saved, and their reward will be eternal life in a place called Paradise. Those who lived a 'bad' life or who did not believe in God or rejected His prophets' teachings will be condemned. Their punishment will be life forever in Hell. Those whose bad deeds outnumber their good deeds will experience Hell for a time, then be allowed to enter Paradise. Although Islamic texts provide several metaphors about what life is like after death, the reality of life after death, as well as Paradise and Hell, is known only to God.

Belief in God's timeless knowledge

Another key belief of Muslims is in God's timeless knowledge. Islam teaches that God knows everything that happens in the universe and He has full knowledge of the past, present and future. Muslims believe that this 'divine knowledge' is recorded.For a Muslim, this means that God has measured out the span of their life—the good things that will happen to each person and the bad things.

The five pillars of Islam

Muslims are expected to perform certain duties called the 'five pillars of Islam'. The five pillars are the central practices of Islam. They define what it means to be a practising Muslim and are foundational to Islam. They are also obligations—things that a Muslim must do. Although Muslims are spread out all over the world, speaking different languages and living in very different contexts, they all have these practices in common. The five pillars of Islam are therefore also a great unifier in the Muslim world.

The declaration of faith

The first pillar of Islam is the testimony and belief that there is no god but God and Muhammad is the messenger of God. Muslims usually declare this in Arabic, saying: '*La ilaha illa Allah, Muhammad rasul Allah*' ('There is no god but God and Muhammad is the messenger of God'). This statement—called the *Shahada*—is the centre of Muslims' faith and actions. Muslims recite it daily as part of their prayers.

Prayer

The second pillar of Islam is prayer. A Muslim is expected to pray at least five times a day. Each prayer involves recitation of parts of the Qur'an and certain movements, such as standing, bending and prostration.

Each of the five prayers or *salat* has a name and is performed at certain times of the day. In Muslim-majority countries, people often know when the time of the prayer comes because the 'call to prayer' is sounded from the local mosque. In Western countries such as Australia, because of council regulations, the call to prayer cannot be heard outside a mosque, so Muslims use other means to remind themselves to pray. When the call to prayer is sounded, observant Muslims usually stop what they are doing and go to pray. Before praying, a Muslim is expected to wash their hands, face, arms and feet in a certain way. This prepares them to meet God in prayer in a clean and pure state.

Muslims can pray anywhere, not just in a mosque. Any place that is clean—such as an office, a classroom or even a park—is suitable. Many Muslims go to the local mosque to pray, but many also choose to pray at home or where they are.

Zakat

The third pillar of Islam is the practice of charitable giving. Muslims are obliged to make charitable payments—called *zakat*—equivalent to 2.5 per cent of one's average annual net savings.

Even though *zakat* is a duty for Muslims, Muslims view it as a form of worship that helps them to be thankful to God for what they have. It also helps them to foster genuine concern for the needy. Many Muslims also choose to give voluntarily at other times. Islam encourages generosity, and stinginess is strongly discouraged.

Fasting

The forth pillar of Islam is the obligation to fast. During Ramadan—the ninth month of the Islamic calendar—all Muslim adults abstain from eating and drinking between dawn and sunset. Fasting during Ramadan is generally a period when Muslims take time to reflect on their lives—to forgive others for their wrongs and make amends for their own misdeeds. It is also one of the most important acts of worship that a Muslim can perform. By fasting, giving up things that one enjoys or needs, a Muslim draws closer to God.

Pilgrimage to Mecca (hajj)

The fifth obligation for a Muslim is to make the pilgrimage or *hajj* to Mecca. At least once in their lifetime, a Muslim who is physically and financially able is expected to perform the pilgrimage during the twelfth month of the Islamic calendar.

Islamic sacred texts

Islam's sacred texts are the Qur'an, the book of the revelation that God sent to the Prophet Muhammad, and *Hadith*, narratives that record aspects of the Prophet's words and actions. Together these texts provide instruction and broad guidance for all aspects of a Muslim's life and the values, ethics and norms of Islam. They also form the foundation of Islamic law.

The Qur'an

The Qur'an is the book of revelation that Muslims believe was sent by God to the Prophet Muhammad through the angel Gabriel over 22 years, between 610 and 632 CE. While the Prophet was alive, he interpreted and passed on these words to the Muslim community and his followers memorised the revelations that he received. Shortly after the Prophet's death, these revelations were compiled into a single volume, called 'the Qur'an'.

The Qur'an has 114 chapters or *suras* of different lengths that are individually named and numbered. Each chapter is further divided into verses or *ayat*. The longest chapter has more than 280 verses, while shortest has only a few verses. Although each chapter has a name, it does not mean that the chapter focuses on the issue or idea the name suggests. In fact, only a handful of verses is likely to be relevant to the name of a given chapter. This means that each chapter, particularly the longer ones, covers a range of topics, ideas and themes. A topic covered in one chapter may be covered in several other chapters. This naturally presents certain difficulties for a reader who is not familiar with the Qur'an.

The entire message of the Qur'an does, however, have certain central themes and concerns. These include God's creation of the universe; His message to human beings; ethical and moral issues such as the evil of injustice and the need to help the poor and disadvantaged; how Muslims should behave in certain circumstances; stories of past prophets; the problems and difficulties faced by the Prophet Muhammad and the first Muslim community; life after death, and Paradise and Hell.

The most often recited chapter of the Qur'an is the first chapter. Muslims read it several times a day, during their prayers. The translation of this chapter means:

> In the name of God, the Most Gracious, the Dispenser of Grace.
> All praise is due to God alone, the Sustainer of all the worlds,
> The Most Gracious, the Dispenser of Grace,
> Lord of the Day of Judgement!
> Thee alone do we worship; and unto Thee alone do we turn for aid.
> Guide us the straight way—
> The way of those upon whom Thou hast bestowed Thy blessings,
> Not of those who have been condemned [by Thee],
> Nor of those who go astray![3]

Given that Muslims understand the Qur'an to be the actual speech of God, they treat it with the utmost respect. A Muslim would therefore not place the Qur'an on the floor or touch its pages with dirty hands, or throw, kick or step on it. These actions are considered a great sacrilege in Islam and are forbidden.

While all Muslims agree that the Qur'an is the Word of God, they have different views and opinions about how it should be interpreted. Some Muslims emphasise a legalistic approach, which means they emphasise the legal texts of the Qur'an, often reading those texts literally, in order to arrive at how God really wants us to behave in particular situations and circumstances. Others take a more mystical approach and look into the text to try to discover deeper spiritual meanings in its metaphors and parables.

There have been many great interpreters of the Qur'an who have written commentaries, called *tafsirs* in Arabic. Each of these authors has taken a different approach to interpreting the Qur'an and has contributed much to the understanding of the Muslim holy book. Today, much as in earlier periods, there are Muslims who are trying to interpret the Qur'an and make it meaningful for Muslims living now. Some Muslims feel that the Qur'an should be interpreted on a continuing basis by each group of people who receive it. In this way, the Qur'an remains always relevant and meaningful. Others argue that the interpretations of early Muslim scholars must be preserved and that Muslims should follow those early interpretations as much as possible.

---

3   Qur'an 1:1–7.

Hadith

The second-most sacred text in Islam is the *Hadith* or the narratives that report the words and deeds of the Prophet Muhammad. During the 22 years of the Prophet's mission, many of the things that the Prophet said and did were told and retold by Muslims, then later documented. The early Muslims used these reports to help them judge how they should live or make decisions after the Prophet's death.

They reasoned that Muslims could learn a lot about how God wanted them to live by following the words and actions of Prophet Muhammad.

The *Hadith* has also been used as an important resource to help Muslims understand what the Qur'an says about different issues. One good example is how Muslims should perform their five daily prayers. The Qur'an commands Muslims to pray but does not give any details about how, when and what form these prayers should take. The Prophet Muhammad explained the daily prayers in detail and showed Muslims how to perform them. These instructions and actions were then recorded in the *Hadith*, which Muslims now rely on when performing their daily prayers.

The *Hadith* that have a reliable chain of narrators stemming back to the Prophet are considered authentic, but not all have this degree of reliability. After the death of the Prophet, many false reports about what he said and did were circulated, which is why the process of authenticating *Hadith* is so important. Muslims rely on historically reliable and authentic *Hadith* to understand the Prophet's practices and guidance.

The *Shari'ah*

Islam began not only as a system of personal beliefs and practices for relating to God, but as a community. The Qur'an and the Prophet introduced a range of rules, regulations and laws to regulate the Muslim community and judge disputes. During the time of the Prophet, leading the Muslim community and judging disputes were simple matters because the Muslim community was small and people could refer to the Prophet directly. After the death of the Prophet in 632 CE, however, the Muslim community expanded into a massive empire and the task became extremely complex. Muslim jurists or scholars began to develop a range of laws for the expanding Muslim empire based on the guidance provided in the Qur'an and the *Hadith*. Their work produced a vast amount of scholarship on all manner of different legal topics, sometimes referred to as the *Shari'ah*. Over time, this body of law has become part of the sacred literature of Muslims and a key reference for all areas of Muslim life and practice.

The body of Islamic law that most Muslim scholars and countries draw on today comes from five extant schools of law, which originated in the first three centuries of Islam. They are named after the leading jurist of each school: Hanafi, Shafi'i, Maliki, Hanbali and Ja'fari. The work of these historic scholars and their followers still has great influence over contemporary Islamic law because Muslim leaders today still consult these legal texts for guidance.

Islamic law or *Shari'ah* is still important today in Muslim-majority countries. While many of the earlier rulings and laws are not applied today in most Muslim countries, there are still a few countries (for example, Saudi Arabia and Iran) that follow closely a large number of those laws.

In most Muslim countries, however, of all the laws developed by early Muslims, it is the laws that are related to family matters (such as marriage, divorce, custody of children, inheritance) that are closely followed. Other areas of law, in general, have been changed or reformed significantly to suit contemporary needs and circumstances, largely as a result of the influence of Western laws and legal systems.

Determining right and wrong

There are two ways by which Muslims usually determine right from wrong. First, Muslims believe that God has provided all people with a faculty to reason, which helps them discern right from wrong. The ability to reason is something that Muslims use to understand what God wants them to do.

Second, God has provided guidance and instructions for all people through His prophets. For Muslims, this guidance is contained in the Qur'an and *Hadith* and is explained further and elaborated on in Islamic law and the principles of Islamic ethics. When a Muslim wants to know whether something is right or wrong, the first question they ask is: 'What does the Qur'an or the Prophet have to say about this?' If there is a clear instruction in the Qur'an or a *Hadith*, a Muslim is encouraged to follow it. For instance, when the Qur'an says 'Do not commit murder', this means that it is wrong to kill a person unlawfully. If the Qur'an is not clear on a specific issue, a Muslim may refer to the *Hadith*, commentaries on the Qur'an or Islamic legal texts or they may ask a local religious leader for advice.

Prohibited foods and other substances

For Muslims, God has specifically prohibited Muslims from eating certain foods. These include pig meat such as ham, pork and bacon or pig fat; the meat of an animal that has died from natural causes or from strangulation or beating; blood (in drinkable form, which is not cooked); and alcoholic drinks such as wine. Muslims are also prohibited from eating food or other substances that are harmful to a person's health.

Perspectives on evil and suffering

Although a person has control over many of his or her actions and in many situations can make a reasonable decision about whether an action will bring about harm or benefit, there is much in the world that cannot be controlled. Some of these circumstances bring good, but others bring misfortune or harm. When a person experiences suffering, the natural response, especially for someone with faith in God, is to ask, 'Why does God allow evil and suffering to exist?'

Throughout Islamic history, Muslim theologians and scholars have also pondered this question. The Qur'an teaches that life is a test and God has given all people a measure of responsibility, so that on the Day of Judgment all will be held responsible for their deeds. Some human beings choose to exercise this responsibility by following the will of God, whereas others reject His way.

Many believe the rejection of God causes sin and suffering to come into the world. Sometimes God allows people to suffer so as to test their patience and steadfastness. The Prophet Job is mentioned in the Qur'an as a believer who suffered greatly but was patient and did not disobey God.

Muslims believe that all that happens in this world is according to God's will. Although God is the only one who knows or can fully understand His will, Muslims believe that everything God does is right, just, good and fair. This gives them confidence to trust in God, even when they are facing circumstances that they do not understand.

Islam also emphasises that there is a life to come after death. This means that everything in this world, including suffering, harm and pain, will come to an end. There is an eternal world without suffering that Muslims believe they can look forward to when they are facing misfortune in this lifetime.

Commonalities and differences between Muslims

Muslims come from different ethnic, cultural and linguistic backgrounds and live in Asia, Africa, Europe, America and Australia. They also speak many different languages, including Arabic, Persian, English, Chinese, Urdu, Spanish, Japanese, German and Russian—to name just a few. With such diversity, it is impossible for all Muslims to think and behave in exactly the same way. Muslims from all over the world do, however, have certain things in common. Core beliefs and practices of Islam are generally agreed on and adhered to by all observant Muslims. These may include the 'five pillars' of Islam, the six articles of belief and the commonly accepted prohibitions—for instance, prohibited foods, murder, theft and adultery. Beyond these there are many differences between Muslims. Some are political or theological; others are just a reflection of the various traditions or practices that differ between cultures.

The difference between Sunni and Shi'a Muslims

The biggest division within Islam is between Sunni and Shi'a Muslims. Historically, this division occurred over the question of who should succeed the Prophet Muhammad. One group of Muslims argued that a family member should be his successor and they nominated his cousin and son-in-law Ali. Those who followed this view came later to be known as Shi'a—meaning a group or supportive party of people. This commonly known term is shortened from the historical '*Shi'at-Ali*', or 'the Party of Ali'.

The majority of the early Muslim community, however, disagreed and nominated as their choice Abu Bakr, the Prophet's close friend and advisor. Those who held this view later came to be known as Sunnis, which came from an Arabic word meaning 'one who follows in the tradition or traditions of the Prophet'.

Abu Bakr was the first ruler and political authority after the death of the Prophet Muhammad. Ali in fact became the fourth ruler. This initial disagreement led over the course of the first 200 years of Islamic history to the emergence of Sunnism and Shi'ism as two groups with their own distinct legal and theological schools and political theories about the rule and governance of the Muslim community. Despite such differences, Sunni and Shi'a Muslims share most of the fundamental beliefs and articles of faith of Islam. Today, the majority of Muslims—about 85 per cent—are Sunnis and approximately 13 per cent of Muslims are Shi'a. Most Muslims of the Shi'a school live in Iran and Iraq, as well as parts of India, Pakistan and Lebanon. Small communities of Shi'a also live elsewhere. Most Muslim-majority countries are Sunni.

Approaches to modern problems

Another area of difference among Muslims is how to approach problems or issues that are unique to our modern times, especially those that have not been addressed explicitly by the Qur'an or the teachings of the Prophet. This is a debate that is not unique to Islam. Members of other religious traditions face this issue too as they seek to 'modernise' their religious traditions to take into account contemporary circumstances but still stay true to their beliefs.

Muslims have different approaches to such issues. Some Muslims are very conservative and tend to want to hold on to 'Islam' as it was practised during the time of the Prophet Muhammad; other Muslims take a more liberal approach and argue that the core principles of the Qur'an should be identified and applied afresh to our modern circumstances. Naturally, there are Muslims who hold views that fit somewhere in between.

Religious authority in Islam

Historically, the idea of having one single religious authority to determine what is acceptable Islamically has not had much support among Muslims, particularly among Sunni Muslims. There is no figure among Muslims that is equivalent to the Pope in Catholicism or a clerical hierarchy, for example, with cardinals or bishops. What this means is that there is no one person, apart from the Prophet Muhammad, who can determine that any particular religious view or teaching is final.

Anyone with knowledge of Islam and related matters can express an opinion on a religious issue. As a result, there is great diversity within Islam and great freedom to hear a range of opinions on religious issues.

In practice, those who have studied Islam and are knowledgeable about the religion do tend to have the strongest say in religious matters. Among the Sunnis, they are referred to as *ulama* or scholars.

Some *ulama* have spent years studying Islam in schools or universities, such as the famous al-Azhar University in Egypt. Others with some knowledge of Islamic theology and law have become influential in the Muslim world because they are 'popular preachers' who use modern media—such as television, radio, video and the Internet—to convey their teachings. Even though technology helps them to do this, their views have no more weight in Islam than those of other Muslims.

Islamic institutions and leaders

Mosques

Mosques are the centres of Muslim communities, where Muslims gather for prayer and fellowship. According to Islamic tradition, the first mosque ever built was the Ka'ba, the black cube-like structure that now stands at the centre of the Sacred Mosque in Mecca, Saudi Arabia. While the Prophet Muhammad was living in Mecca, he used the building as his principal mosque and performed prayers there. After the Prophet and his followers migrated to Medina, they built a mosque there that functioned as the centre of the community's activities, including worship.

Mosques are usually used as a place of prayer, particularly the five daily prayers led by a prayer leader called an *imam*. In addition to the daily prayers, mosques often hold regular Friday prayer—called *Jum'ah*—which replaces the midday prayer on Friday.

Mosques also provide a focus for the Muslim obligation to give charity. During Ramadan, some mosques host *iftar* dinners so the congregation can break the fast together. The poorer members of the area are invited to participate and the local community is encouraged to bring food along to share as a way of being thankful and providing charity for those in need. Some mosques also help collect *zakat* and distribute it to the disadvantaged.

In accordance with Islamic teachings, mosques comply with certain religious requirements. While some of these are universal to all mosques, others vary from mosque to mosque. All mosques have rules about cleanliness because it is an important prerequisite for worship. Shoes, for example, are kept outside the entrance to the mosque building.

As mosques are places of worship, visitors and congregants must be respectful towards those who are praying. Loud conversation is discouraged and it is considered unacceptable to interrupt people while they are praying. Likewise, rules about the separation of men and women are also designed, according to many Muslims, to prevent distractions. In many mosques, men and women pray in different parts of the prayer hall—usually one half for men and the other half for women. Sometimes mosques have a special railed-off section for women or a barrier or partition to separate them from the male congregants. The Grand Mosque of Mecca, however, which is the most sacred place for Muslims, has no such separate sections for men and women.

Mosques have different rules about whether or not non-Muslims are allowed to visit. Traditionally, non-Muslims were allowed to go inside mosques, as long as they did not eat or sleep in the building or disturb the congregants. Today, many mosques allow non-Muslims to visit at certain times as long as they are appropriately covered.

Islam and contentious issues

Treatment of women

Islam is often depicted as a religion that oppresses women. Practices that discriminate against women, such as strict segregation, veiling or polygamous marriages, are often highlighted, particularly by the media, leading to the view that all Muslims oppress or discriminate against women. This assumption is sometimes encouraged further by reports of how Muslim women are treated in some Muslim-majority countries or by stories that girls are discouraged from attending school in a few Muslim communities or that women are forbidden to engage in mundane activities such as driving a car. It is understandable therefore that many people believe that Muslims have a poor view of women. Similar to many other matters in Islam, however, Muslims hold a wide variety of different views on practices that concern women.

In many Muslim societies, women and men are considered equal before the law. Both have access to education and employment and participate in the political system. In some majority-Muslim states, women have even held the highest office in the country—for example, women have been prime ministers or heads of state in Indonesia, Pakistan, Bangladesh and Turkey, which are among the largest Muslim countries.

Women do, however, face systematic discrimination in numerous Muslim societies. Much of this comes from longstanding cultural practices, values and norms, although it is commonly justified using religious arguments. For many Muslim women, challenging discriminatory practices and perspectives is an important part of their struggle for justice, and many find the strength and ability to do it by appealing to Islamic texts, values and principles, not by renouncing Islam.

These women strongly believe that Islam itself does not oppress women; however, interpretations of key religious texts have led to discriminatory practices. For them, these interpretations can be questioned and revised.

Polygyny

Although polygyny is widely associated with Islam, it is practised only in some majority-Muslim countries. For example, Tunisia, Bosnia-Herzegovina and Turkey all ban the practice. In Indonesia, the country with the largest Muslim population in the world, the practice is strictly regulated and additional marriages often require court permission before they can be registered. Saudi Arabia, on the other hand, allows polygyny and imposes few restrictions.

Attitudes towards polygyny in Muslim countries are influenced by local cultural norms and practices. In societies where polygyny has been widely practised in the past—such as Saudi Arabia or some West African countries—it is more common and more accepted than in countries where the practice is relatively new or uncommon. Historically, many cultures have practiced polygyny—not just Muslims or Arabs.

The Prophet Muhammad himself had a monogamous marriage with his wife, Khadijah, for 25 years, until she passed away. At that time, polygyny was not at all unusual, and after Khadijah's death, the Prophet married a number of other women—mostly for political and charitable reasons. Muslims believe that the Prophet Muhammad had special permission to marry these wives. They were all called the 'Mothers of the Believers' and were cared for by the Muslim community after the Prophet passed away.

Today, polygyny is permitted under traditional Islamic law but with certain restrictions. A man may take only up to four wives, no more. The Qur'an also states that any man who wishes to enter into a polygamous relationship must consider first whether he can treat each of his wives fairly. This means spending equal amounts of time and money on them, housing them with the same standard of living and providing equally for any children of the marriages. The Qur'an insists that if a man is not able to do this he should not enter into any further marriages.

Even though polygyny is permitted in Islam, there is debate among Muslim scholars about whether it should still be allowed today. Many scholars argue that polygyny used to have a specific purpose in that it was necessary in the early years of Islam to take care of orphans or widows who had no economic means if the male breadwinner of the household was killed in war or died. Conditions, however, and therefore the need, are not the same today. Other scholars maintain that since polygyny is permitted in Islam it cannot be banned, regardless of the changes that have taken place in society.

Islam and violence

Many people believe that Islam is a religion that teaches violence against non-Muslims and that, compared with people of other faiths, Muslims are more likely to be violent and intolerant.

This belief might stem from negative images that existed about Islam and Muslims in medieval Europe. For example, in Europe at the time, Muslims were thought falsely to be barbaric, violent and fanatical—an image that has continued into the twenty-first century. The perception has also been reinforced by the actions of a few Muslims who have violated the most fundamental precepts of the religion, such as those who carried out the terrorist attacks on New York and Washington, DC, on 11 September 2001, the Bali bombings in October 2002 and the London bombings of 2005.

In many religious traditions, there are those who have resorted to violence to achieve religious or political objectives, including among Muslims. History records violent and fanatical actions by adherents to a number of faiths, including Catholics, Protestants, Jews, Hindus and Buddhists. Like people of other faiths, however, the majority of Muslims do not advocate or use violence and wish to live peacefully with other people. The Qur'an stresses that conversion to Islam by force is against the religion and such conversions are invalid. Indeed, '[t]here is no compulsion in religion'.[4] For the majority of Muslims, Islam is a religion of peace that encourages peaceful and harmonious relations with others. Instead of condoning violence or terrorism, most Muslims reject these actions.

---

4   2:256.

12. The position of Tibet in international law

VENERABLE ALEX BRUCE,
THE AUSTRALIAN NATIONAL UNIVERSITY

Tibet's story is that of an ancient nation hurled into the twentieth century by the loss of its sovereignty.[1]

Introduction

During the 2008 Beijing Olympic Summer Games, many news stories carried disturbing images of protesters scuffling with police and security guards at different sporting venues within China. Even before the games began, protesters interrupted the Olympic torch relay and we saw images of Chinese security forces in blue tracksuits jogging beside the torch in order to protect it from protesters. At one point, the torch had to be carried on a bus through one location for its own protection.

Perhaps the greatest controversy surrounding the torch relay was the decision by the Chinese Government to send it through Tibet. In fact, most of the protests surrounding the torch relay concerned China's troubled relationship with Tibet. We saw banners concerning the plight of Tibet unfurled from the Golden Gate Bridge in San Francisco and from the steps of the Opera House in Sydney, Australia.

Why were these protests so virulent? What exactly is the situation concerning China's relationship with Tibet that arouses so much anger in the West? The People's Republic of China (PRC) claims that Tibet has always been and remains a part of China. As such, the protests concerning Tibet are viewed as an unjustified interference in the 'internal affairs' of China. China claims that it 'liberated' part of its own territory from colonial 'imperialists' when its army occupied Tibet in 1959.

---

1   Avedon, J. 1979, *In Exile From the Land of Snows,* Wisdom Publications, Boston, p. xiii.

The international community, however, disagrees. Research into the position of Tibet in international law seems to be voluminous and largely settled in concluding that at the time of the Chinese occupation, Tibet enjoyed sovereign statehood status.

If that is correct then the Chinese military's occupation of Tibet was and continues to be illegal. And when the many documented instances of human rights abuses in Tibet by China are factored into the issue, the situation within Tibet appears grim.

The 'Tibet issue' is confusing for many people. What is the basis of China's claims that Tibet is part of China? What does His Holiness the Dalai Lama have to say about China's claims? And what about the international community; what does international law have to say about the Tibet issue?

In this chapter, I would like to present an overview of these issues and explain the positions of China and the international community.

After studying the facts and the international legal framework concerning China's actions, it is difficult to avoid the conclusion that while scholars of international law recognise the *theoretical* right of the Tibetan people to self-determination to the point of independence from China, the reality is that no state will seek to enforce international law against China.

The reasons for this are prudential—motivated largely by economic self-interest in exploiting China's massive and relatively untouched markets and the lack of practical enforcement options open to the international community given China's power in the United Nations, and particularly its presence on the Security Council.

In addition, China's attitude towards negotiations with the Tibetans is characterised by suspicion, hostility and belligerence towards what it calls the 'Dalai clique'. In 2008, this culminated with the absurd accusation that His Holiness had devised an elaborate plan to sabotage the 2008 Beijing Olympics.

I am well aware that as a Buddhist monk generally, and a monk ordained into the Tibetan Buddhist tradition of His Holiness the Dalai Lama specifically, my views are vulnerable to allegations of bias and partiality. I hope, however, to demonstrate that the views expressed in this chapter are well researched and independently supported by other scholars of greater abilities than myself.

Tibet in international law

Scholarly research into the position of Tibet in international law seems to be voluminous and largely settled in concluding that at the time of the Chinese occupation in 1950, Tibet enjoyed sovereign statehood status. As Sloane notes:

> The answer [to the Tibet question] is not that Tibet's status is 'debateable'. To my knowledge, without exception, every independent scholar who has examined this question concluded that Tibet qualified under international law as a sovereign state in 1950, the year during which the People's Liberation Army invaded and colonised Tibet.[2]

As far back as 1954, international scholarship concluded that Tibet was an independent state.[3] Each decade since the 1950 occupation of Tibet has produced further scholarship reaching identical conclusions.[4]

These conclusions have also been reflected in the determinations of various private and public legal bodies, such as the International Commission of Jurists and the Unrepresented Nations and Peoples Organisation (UNPO).[5]

Predictably, Chinese scholarship, also since 1950, vigorously disputes these conclusions. Tieh-Tseng Li relies on the content of the various instruments 'voluntarily adopted' by Tibet after 1950 as evidence of China's sovereignty over Tibet.[6]

For example, the Peking Agreement on Measures for the Peaceful Liberation of Tibet signed in May 1951 states: 'The Tibetan people shall unite, drive out imperial aggressive forces from Tibet and return to the big family of the Motherland—the People's Republic of China.'[7]

Equally predictably, Western legal scholarship has attacked the validity of the agreement in international law.

---

2   Sloane, R. 2002, 'The changing face of international recognition in international law', *Emory International Law Review*, vol. 16, no. 107, p. 131.
3   Alexandrowicz, C. H. 1954, 'The legal position of Tibet', *American Journal of International Law*, vol. 48, no. 2, p. 265.
4   Rubin, A. 1968, 'The position of Tibet in international law', *The China Quarterly*, vol. 35, p. 110; Christie, C. 1976, 'Great Britain, China and the status of Tibet', *Modern Asian Studies*, vol. 10, p. 481; Walt van Pragg, M. 1988, 'The legal status of Tibet', *Cultural Survival Quarterly*, vol. 12, p. 67; Norbu, D. 1997, 'Tibet in Sino–Indian relations', *Asian Survey*, vol. 37, no. 11, p. 1078; Clark, R. 2002, 'China's unlawful control over Tibet', *Indiana International & Comparative Law Review*, vol. 12, p. 293.
5   International Commission of Jurists 1997, *Tibet: Human rights and the rule of law*, December, International Commission of Jurists, Geneva; Unrepresented Nations and Peoples Organisation (UNPO) 1996, *The Question of Self-Determination: The case of East Timor, Tibet and Western Sahara*, Conference report, 25–26 March 1996, Geneva.
6   Tieh-Tseng Li 1956, 'The legal position of Tibet', *The American Journal of International Law*, vol. 50, no. 2, p. 394.
7   Ibid., p. 403.

This 'agreement', which is also known as the 'Seventeen-Point Agreement', was signed at gunpoint while Chinese troops occupied Lhasa, the capital of Tibet. It was signed by Tibetan representatives who did not have the capacity to sign such an agreement, and the Tibetans were given no time to consult with the '*Kashag*' (the Tibetan parliament) or the Dalai Lama.

For this reason, the Chinese 'negotiation' team forged the seal of the Tibetan Government. It was forged because at the time it was allegedly affixed, the genuine seal was with the *Kashag* and the Dalai Lama, who had fled Lhasa after being shelled by Chinese troops.[8]

In these circumstances, international-law scholars have vehemently denounced the legality of the agreement and the circumstances in which it was forced on the Tibetan people.[9]

This seemingly obvious conclusion did not stop the Chinese Government from 'celebrating' the fiftieth anniversary of the Seventeen-Point Agreement in May 2001. Chinese propaganda notified Tibetans living in Lhasa that '[p]articipation in the celebrations is an important political responsibility'.[10]

More recent Chinese scholarship characterises Tibet as an underdeveloped and exploited part of China that has experienced unprecedented economic growth and prosperity since its 'peaceful liberation' by the Chinese Army in 1950.[11]

Lack of 'middle-ground' scholarship

There is very little scholarship that meets in the middle. While the *tone* of recent scholarship is less polemical than in the past, written in an attempt to seek 'resolutions' to the 'Tibet issue',[12] the starting point remains the assumed sovereignty of Tibet before 1950. This is not surprising given that more than 50 years of international scholarship apparently reaches the same conclusion.

Another reason might be what Sautman describes as an 'émigré discourse… framed in the starkest terms in order to force the hand of international elites [preventing] the PRC's plan to "crush an ancient civilisation"'.[13]

It is true that in the West, discourse on Tibet often starts from an *a priori* assumption that Tibet was a veritable 'Shangri-la' crushed by China, whose

---

8 Laird, T. 2006, *The Story of Tibet*, Grove Press, United States, p. 310.
9 Ibid.; Clark, 'China's unlawful control over Tibet', pp. 300–1.
10 Tibet Information Network, <http://www.tibetinfo.net/news-updates/nu030501.htm>
11 Yan Hao 2000, 'Tibetan population in China: myths and facts re-examined', *Asian Ethnicity*, vol. 1, p. 11.
12 Misra, A. 2000, 'Tibet: in search of a resolution', *Central Asian Survey*, vol. 19, no. 1, p. 79.
13 Sautman, B. 2003, '"Cultural genocide" and Tibet', *Texas International Law Journal*, vol. 38, p. 175.

intentions were nothing less than the destruction of the Tibetan culture. In contemporary Western culture, the Tibetan cause is fashionable; several high-profile identities in the entertainment industry, including Harrison Ford, Richard Gere and Keanu Reeves, lend star appeal to the Tibetan 'émigré discourse'.[14]

The real issue does not seem to involve the legal status of Tibet pre-1950 (a matter studied exhaustively) or what form of autonomous government might best enable Tibet to enjoy some degree of self-determination—a subject also well studied, particularly by scholars Eva Herzer and Michael Walt van Praag.[15]

Perhaps for this reason, the majority of recent scholarship concerning Tibet focuses not on issues of state recognition or self-determination, but on the many human rights abuses perpetrated by China in its continuing occupation of Tibet.[16]

Again, there is much scholarship concerning China's human rights record in Tibet, indicating systematic contraventions of just about every human rights declaration, covenant and convention that exists—many of which China is a signatory to.

For example, the 1997 report of the International Commission of Jurists' investigation of Tibet found that China had committed and continued to engage in arbitrary arrest and detention, torture and ill treatment, extra-judicial and arbitrary executions, forced abortions, forced sterilisation of women, systematic discrimination against Tibetans in housing, education and employment as well as denying freedom of expression, assembly and religious worship.[17]

The 'real' question to ask

When these findings are added to the apparent unanimity of international scholarship concerning Tibet's status in international law, the pivotal question is why the international community permits China to continue its military occupation of Tibet and accompanying widespread, documented human rights abuses?

---

14 Paine, J. 2004, *Re-Enchantment: Tibetan Buddhism comes to the West*, W. W. Norton & Company, United States.
15 Herzer, E. 2000, *Options for Tibet's Future Political Status*, Tibetan Parliamentary and Policy Research Centre, New Delhi, India.
16 Craig, M. 1992, *Tears of Blood: A cry for Tibet*, HarperCollins, London; Laird, *The Story of* Tibet.
17 International Commission of Jurists, *Tibet*, pp. 204–305.

This is the question posed by Sloane:

> Today, few dispute that illegal occupation cannot of itself terminate statehood. For this reason the international community rightly objected to Iraq's attempt to annex Kuwait in 1990, to the Soviet Union's invasion of Afghanistan in 1979 and to Indonesia's purported annexation of East Timor in 1975. Why then does every State continue to validate China's sovereignty over Tibet when its only conceivable claim, as shown repeatedly by historical and international scholarship, is military annexation?

The answer is relatively simple and is provided by Sloane himself:

> The unsurprising reason that no state recognises the State of Tibet is that it had the misfortune to be invaded by a powerful state and at a time when the international community's attention was diverted elsewhere. Today, China is a nuclear power, it exercises a veto as a permanent member of the UN Security Council and economically, it has become…a tremendous market that States feel they cannot afford to neglect by antagonizing China's political elite. Political realism and economic self-interest in short, motivate states' formal recognition practices towards China's assertion of sovereignty over Tibet.[18]

Balancing the need to be seen as a responsible international citizen with the need to extend and preserve economic self-interest has therefore led many states into linguistic contortions in expressing their attitude towards Tibet.

For example, the US Department of State's *Country Reports on Human Rights Practices* provides:

> The United States recognises the Tibet Autonomous Region (TAR)—hereinafter referred to as 'Tibet'—to be part of the People's Republic of China. The preservation and development of Tibet's unique religious, cultural and linguistic heritage and protection of its people's fundamental human rights continue to be of concern.[19]

On the one hand, the report recognises that Tibet is part of the People's Republic of China. On the other hand, the report acknowledges that the Tibetans are not Chinese and are not a subset of the Chinese people. In the meantime, the United States (and other Western countries) extends varying degrees of hospitality to the Dalai Lama all the while fending off vigorous protests from the Chinese Government.

---

18   Sloane, 'The changing face of international recognition in international law', pp. 131–2.
19   US Department of State 2000, *Country Reports on Human Rights Practices,* February 2001, United States Department of State, Washington, DC.

Tibetans and the right to self-determination

If international legal scholarship concerning Tibet's status in international law is correct, and if the numerous fact-finding committees' conclusions concerning continuing gross human rights violations by China are also correct, do the Tibetans have the right to secede from China as part of a right to self-determination?

This question concerns the issue of whether the Tibetans are a 'people' with the right to internal and external self-determination.

Article 1 of the UN Charter states that one of its purposes is to 'develop friendly relations among nations based on respect for the principle of equal rights and self-determination of peoples'.

Traditionally, the United Nations developed the right to self-determination within the Western decolonisation context, starting with the Declaration on the Granting of Independence to Colonial Countries and Peoples.[20] Since 1960, the right to self-determination has been recognised as an absolute norm of general international law amounting to *jus cogens*. The International Court of Justice in the East Timor case stated: 'the right of peoples to self-determination, as it evolved from the Charter and from United Nations Practice, has an *erga omnes* character.'[21]

With time, the principle was developed and articulated in further instruments. For example, the Declaration on Principles of International Law concerning Friendly Relations and Co-Operation Among States ('the Friendly Relations Declaration') defines self-determination to mean:

> By virtue of the principle of equal rights and self-determination of peoples enshrined in the Charter of the United Nations, all peoples have the right freely to determine, without external interference, their political status and to pursue their economic, social and cultural development, and every State has the duty to respect this right in accordance with the provisions of the Charter.[22]

---

20 United Nations 1960, *Declaration on the Granting of Independence to Colonial Countries and Peoples*, General Assembly Resolution 1514 (XV), 14 December 1960, United Nations, New York.
21 International Court of Justice 1995, *East Timor (Portugal vs Australia)*, Report 90, 30 June, International Court of Justice, The Hague,
The Netherlands, p. 102.
22 United Nations 1970, *Declaration on Principles of International Law concerning Friendly Relations and Co-Operation Among States in Accordance with the Charter of the United Nations*, General Assembly Resolution 2625, UN Doc A/8028, United Nations, New York, p. 121.

Most international instruments concerning economic, political and human rights affirm that self-determination is a legal right: 'All peoples have the right to self-determination. By virtue of this right, they freely determine their political status and freely pursue their economic, social and cultural development.'[23]

Tibetans as a 'people'

Self-determination accrues to a group recognised as a 'people' by international law.[24] While it might be difficult to define a 'people' in the abstract, indices adopted by the UN Educational, Scientific and Cultural Organisation (UNESCO) in 1990 include a common historical tradition, racial or ethnic identity, cultural homogeneity, linguistic unity, religious affinity, territorial connections and a common economic field.[25]

Relying on the UNESCO indices, the Permanent Tribunal of Peoples[26] and the Conference of International Lawyers on Issues Relating to Self-Determination and Independence for Tibet[27] concluded that Tibetans met the international law criteria for 'people' and were entitled to exercise their right to self-determination.

In 1961, the UN General Assembly passed a resolution calling for 'the cessation of practices which deprive the Tibetan people of their fundamental human rights and freedoms, including the right to self-determination'.[28]

The existence of continuing human rights abuses perpetrated against Tibetans is of special significance in the context of the right to self-determination. This is because an internal right to human rights protection and an external right to freedom from domination are incorporated into the right to self-determination.[29]

---

23 United Nations 1966, *International Covenant on Economic, Social and Cultural Rights(ICESR). Part 1*, General Assembly Resolution 2200, United Nations, New York; United Nations 1966, *International Covenant on Civil and Political Rights(ICCPR). Part 2*, General Assembly Resolution 2200, United Nations, New York.
24 Simpson, G. 1996, 'The diffusion of sovereignty: self determination in the post-colonial age', *Stanford Journal of International Law*, vol. 32, p. 255.
25 United Nations Educational, Scientific and Cultural Organisation (UNESCO) 1990, *International Meeting of Experts on Further Study of the Concept of the Rights of Peoples: Final report and recommendations*, UNESCO, Paris.
26 Permanent Tribunal of Peoples 1992, *Session on Tibet: verdict*, Permanent Tribunal of Peoples, Strasbourg, France, p. 14.
27 Conference of International Lawyers on Issues Relating to Self-Determination and Independence for Tibet 1993, *The Position of Tibet in International Law*, Conference of International Lawyers on Issues Relating to Self-Determination and Independence for Tibet, London.
28 United Nations 1961, General Assembly Resolution 1723 (XVI), United Nations, New York.
29 Radin, M. 1993, 'The right to self determination as a mechanism for group autonomy: protection of Tibetan cultural rights', *Washington Law Review*, vol. 68, p. 706.

Kolonder points out that the internal right to self-determination is the entitlement to human rights protection, which 'entitles a people to participate effectively in the decision-making process which affects the political, economic, social and cultural conditions under which it lives'.[30]

When it examined the status of Tibet in December 1997, the International Commission of Jurists specifically recognised that pervasive and continuing human rights abuses by China represented a violation of the Tibetan peoples' right to self-determination:

> The content of the right of self-determination was further developed in the 1970 *'Declaration on Principles of International Law concerning Friendly Relations and Cooperation among States'*. The principle of equal rights and self-determination of peoples, in particular, clarifies that 'subjugation of peoples to alien subjugation, domination and exploitation constitutes a violation of the principle'.[31]

Therefore, as a norm of international law, the right to self-determination accrues to a 'people' who are under colonial domination and subject to exploitation as well as to people under alien subjugation and exploitation.

Internal self-determination does not equate to external secession

Even if the Tibetans are recognised as a 'people' in international law, the right to self-determination does not carry with it the right to secession. As Radin notes: 'Under modern international law, the right of peoples to self determination does not presume a right to secession, but rather aims at the establishment of internal conditions for the enjoyment of all human rights.'[32]

It is therefore clear that the right to self-determination is subject to limits also recognised by international law, including territorial integrity and the doctrine of *uti possidetis juris*.[33] In particular, the Friendly Relations Declaration states:

> Nothing in the foregoing paragraphs shall be construed as authorising or encouraging any action which would dismember or impair, totally or in part, the territorial integrity or political unity of sovereign and independent States conducting themselves in compliance with the

---

30 Kolonder, E. 1994, 'The future of the right to self-determination', *Connecticut Journal of International Law*, vol. 10, p. 159.
31 International Commission of Jurists, *Tibet*, p. 322.
32 Radin, 'The right to self determination as a mechanism for group autonomy', p. 705.
33 Sforza, J. 1999, 'The Timor Gap dispute: the validity of the Timor Gap Treaty, self determination and decolonisation', *Suffolk Transnational Law Review*, vol. 22, p. 515.

principle of equal rights and self-determination of peoples and this possessed of a government representing the whole people belonging to a territory without distinction as to race, creed or colour.[34]

The consequences of this extract from the Friendly Relations Declaration for Tibet are stark; if Tibet has always been a part of China then there is unlikely to be a right of secession.

If, however, Tibet was an independent state in 1950 at the time of the Chinese military incursion, two possibilities present themselves. First, China's invasion of Tibet breached international law and its continuing presence in Tibet represents an unlawful occupation. Second, the Tibetans' right to self-determination may ultimately be viewed through the lens of 'alien subjugation'.

Tibetans under alien subjugation or simply part of China?

It is generally recognised that the right to self-determination has two aspects: an 'internal' and an 'external' aspect. These aspects were explained in a 1996 General Comment adopted by the UN Committee on the Elimination of Racial Discrimination:

> In respect of the self-determination of peoples, two aspects have to be distinguished. The right to self-determination of peoples has an internal aspect, ie., the rights of all peoples to pursue freely their economic, social and cultural development without outside interference...The external aspect of self-determination implies that all peoples have the right to determine freely their political status and their place in the international community based upon the principle of equal rights and exemplified by the liberation of peoples from colonialism and by the prohibition to subject peoples to alien subjugation, domination and exploitation.[35]

One of the many difficulties associated with the status of Tibet in international law, however, lies precisely in its complicated historical relationship with China. China maintains that Tibet has always been part of its territory and therefore the argument that Tibet is 'subject to alien domination' is unfounded.

---

34   United Nations, General Assembly Resolution 2625, United Nations, New York, para. 7.
35   UN Committee on the Elimination of Racial Discrimination 1996, General Recommendation XXI (48), 8 March 1996, United Nations, New York.

China points to the Peking Agreement on Measures for the Peaceful Liberation of Tibet signed in May 1951, which states: 'The Tibetan people shall unite, drive out imperial aggressive forces from Tibet and return to the big family of the Motherland—the People's Republic of China.'

China asserts that it makes

> [n]o claims to sovereign rights over Tibet as a result of its military subjugation and occupation of Tibet following the country's annexation or prescription in this period. Instead, it bases its claim to Tibet solely on the theory that Tibet has been an integral part of China for centuries.[36]

In fact, the Chinese Communist Party maintains that China has exercised control over Tibet since the Yuan Dynasty (1271–1368).[37] For this reason, China consistently attacks any attempt by the international community to investigate the Tibet issue as interference in the internal affairs of the People's Republic of China.

China's assertion of control over Tibet since the thirteenth century also demonstrates that debate about the sovereignty of Tibet and its complicated historical relationship with China is long and complex. As Crawford notes:

> In 1910, Tibet possessed a considerable degree of *defacto* independence but this was conditioned by Chinese power with respect to Tibetan foreign affairs, and by the claims of China (largely unexercised) to some degree of control. By 1911 the Manchu dynasty collapsed, with it, it has been argued, collapsed also the claims of China over Tibet since these were based on a personal allegiance under feudal law.[38]

The consequences are very significant, for as Walt van Pragg observes: 'If Tibet is under unlawful Chinese occupation, China's illegal presence in the country is a legitimate object of international concern. If on the other hand, Tibet is an integral part of China, then these questions fall, as China claims, within its own domestic jurisdiction.'[39]

The answer to this question is very much a threshold determinant; sovereignty does not become an issue if Tibet always was and continues to be part of China. Part of the difficulty in answering the question lies in attempts to 'fit' Western European concepts of statehood, sovereignty and colonialism into an Eastern cultural context.

---

36 Walt van Pragg, *The Legal Status of Tibet*, p. 67.
37 McKay, A. (ed.) 2003, *The History of Tibet. Volume III. The modern period: 1895–1959*, Routledge Curzon, London.
38 Crawford, J. 2006, *The Creation of States in International Law*, Second edn, Oxford University Press, Oxford, p. 326.
39 Walt van Pragg, *The Legal Status of Tibet*, p. 67.

Much scholarship of international law has been devoted to establishing whether Tibet 'satisfies' the four basic requirements of the Montevideo Convention on the Rights and Duties of States for recognition as an independent state: a permanent population, defined territory, effective government and a capacity to enter into foreign relations.[40]

In fact, the 1960 Legal Commission of Jurists' Legal Inquiry Committee on Tibet concluded that between 1913 and 1950, Tibet demonstrated the conditions of statehood as accepted in international law.[41]

1. In 1950, there was a Tibetan people and a territory.
2. There was a functioning government (the *Kashag*) conducting its own domestic affairs free from outside authority.
3. Foreign relations in Tibet were conducted exclusively by the Government of Tibet between 1913 and 1950 with foreign countries whose own documents demonstrate that they regarded Tibet as an independent state.

There are, however, difficulties with the cogency of this analysis. The relationship between Tibet and China was never the product of Western juridical categories. It is sometimes difficult therefore to bring methods grounded in Western international law to a determination of Tibet's status. As Sloane observes:

> To assert that Tibet qualified as an independent state in 1950 does not imply that Tibet was always an independent state; nor, however, does it confirm that Tibet was always a part of China. In fact, in a strong sense, both sides of the argument suffer from a categorical mistake. The distinctly modern Western conception of the nation-state, with precise borders and a single centralised government is probably inapposite to pre-twentieth century China and Tibet alike.[42]

While it is true that as at 1950 Tibet possessed characteristics of what Western international law required for state recognition, the precise relationship between Tibet and China was far more fluid. In fact, the relationship was characterised by the term '*cho-yon*'—a term that recognised a religious relationship of priest–patron that included the implied recognition of Tibet's '*suzerainty*', roughly translated as a level of self-governance between de jure and de facto independence.[43]

---

40 Chung, W. 2000, 'Obtaining "state" status: Tibet's uncertain future', *Touro International Law Review*, vol. 10, p. 307.
41 International Commission of Jurists 1960, *Legal Inquiry Committee on Tibet*, International Commission of Jurists, Geneva.
42 Sloane, 'The changing face of recognition in international law', n. 86, p. 107.
43 International Commission of Jurists, *Tibet*, p. 333.

These relational terms do not find their equivalent in Western international law, and for this reason, Walt van Pragg cautions: 'The student of Tibet's past legal status inevitably confronts the problem of finding legal categories and terms appropriate to describe and define the position of this Central Asian country in relation to its neighbours.'[44]

It is accepted that category confusion can hinder the evaluation of Tibet's status in international law. As at 1950, however, Tibet was not so isolated from the world that international legal jurisprudence could not understand the nature of Tibet, its culture, people, territory and government.

As this brief discussion has indicated, international legal scholarship since the early 1950s has consistently reached the conclusion that Tibet was at least a de facto state operating independently of China—and especially of Mao's Communist Party, which gained control in 1949.

Clark sums up the overwhelming conclusion of international legal scholarship since 1950:

> The best remedy for the Tibetan people would be for China to recognise Tibet's right to self determination and allow them to secede from China. This is an egregious case in which Tibet should be able to break free from China's rule and become independent in order to protect the Tibetan's interest in their own lives. By exercising this right, the Tibetans will live in a more peaceful world, and the number of human rights violations that are occurring in Chinese-occupied Tibet will decrease.[45]

'External' right to self-determination

There is an intimate relationship between the concepts of internal and external rights to self-determination posited by the 1996 General Comment adopted by the UN Committee on the Elimination of Racial Discrimination outlined above. The form and structure of the external right to self-determination are intended to facilitate the internal right to self-determination.

The process can be explained as follows, relying on Kolonder's analysis. First, the internal right to self-determination is the entitlement to human rights protection, which 'entitles a people to participate effectively in the decision making process which affects the political, social and cultural conditions under which it lives'.[46]

---

44 Quoted by Sloane in 'The changing face of recognition in international law', n. 85, p. 107.
45 Clark, 'China's unlawful control over Tibet', p. 328.
46 Kolonder, 'The future of the right to self-determination', p. 326.

Second, the external right to self-determination is the freedom from domination that 'entitles a people to decide its international identity and to be free from foreign influence which affects the international status of that state'.[47]

Each form of the right to self-determination reflects an expression of the will and desires of the peoples involved. As the International Court of Justice in the Western Sahara case stated, 'the application of the right to self-determination requires a free and genuine expression of the will of the peoples concerned'.[48]

This is consistent with many international-law instruments—for example, Article 21(3) of the Universal Declaration of Human Rights states: 'the will of the people shall be the bases of the authority of government; this will shall be expressed in periodic and genuine elections which shall be by universal and equal suffrage and shall be held by secret vote or by equivalent free voting procedures.'[49]

Accordingly, the Universal Declaration of Human Rights anticipates that the classical means to ascertain the desire and will of the people is the holding of elections or referendums under conditions ensuring a free and fair outcome. This is notoriously difficult for a people under alien subjugation:

> A people under colonial and alien domination is unable to express its will freely in a consultation, plebiscite or referendum organised and controlled exclusively by the colonial or alien power. Only when it is really and genuinely free is the expression of a people's will capable of determining the politico-international status of the people in question.[50]

Tibet's 'settler' problem

The very significant yet under-examined problem faced by Tibet in the unlikely event that China permitted a referendum is the issue of population transfer. As Pomerance asks: 'How can a legitimate consultation of the wishes of a people be reconciled with respecting the rights of an alien settler population that may outnumber the original population of the territory?'[51]

---

47   Ibid., p. 327.
48   International Court of Justice 1975, *Western Saharacase,* ICJ Reports, International Court of Justice, The Hague, The Netherlands, para. 55.
49   United Nations 1948, *Universal Declaration of Human Rights,* 10 December 1948, United Nations, New York, Article 21(3).
50   International Commission of Jurists, *Tibet,* p. 340.
51   Pomerance, M. 1982, *Self Determination in Law and Practice,* Martinus Nijhoff Publishers, The Hague, p. 29.

In 2007, construction of the US$4 billion Qinghai–Tibet railroad was completed. It is the highest railroad in the world, with trains running at 5072 metres above sea level. Labourers had to wear oxygen masks and bottles while constructing the track.

The railroad is simply a means for China to continue its policy of diluting the ethnic Tibetan population, effectively forcing Tibetans into becoming a minority within their own country. China has a well-established policy of ethnic dilution. For example, after completing the railroad to Hohot in the 1920s, ethnic Han Chinese were quickly resettled in Mongolia, ensuring an 11-to-one Han majority by 1949.[52] Likewise, China completed a railroad to Urumqi in Muslim-dominated Xinjiang Province, which effected a 30 per cent increase in the ethnic Han make-up of the province.[53]

In 1952, two years after the Chinese invasion of Tibet, Mao Zedong himself issued the Directive of the Central Committee of the CPC on Policies for Work in Tibet.[54] This directive proposed a fivefold increase in the population of Tibet— by Han Chinese. Mao was alleged to have remarked that he wished to see Tibet's population increase to a level of 10 million Han Chinese.

In 1985, the Chinese Embassy in New Delhi, India, announced that the Chinese Communist Party intended to '[c]hange both the ecological imbalance and population lack in Tibet…migration should be welcomed by the local population and should result in a population increase of sixty million and maybe even a hundred million in less than thirty years'.[55]

Despite Article 49 of the Fourth Geneva Convention, which prohibits any occupying power deporting or transferring parts of its own civilian population into the territory it occupies, China has carried out its intention to 'correct the ecological imbalance' and to transfer large numbers of ethnic Han Chinese into Tibet to do so.

Presenting a report to the 1992 UNPO Conference on Population Transfer, Tibetan representative Lodi Gyari noted that for three decades from 1950 to 1980, the Han Chinese population transfer to Tibet was centrally planned and

---

52   Haertling, P. 2007, 'Trains above the clouds: the primacy of political and civil human rights in Tibet and the People's Republic of China', *Colorado Journal of International Environmental Law and Policy*, vol. 18, p. 472.
53   Ibid.
54   Central Tibetan Administration 1996, *Population Transfer and Control*, Central Tibetan Administration, McLeod Ganj, Dharamsala, India, <http://www.tibet.net>
55   Embassy of the People's Republic of China 1985, *Movement Westward*, ref no. 2, Embassy of the People's Republic of China, New Delhi, India.

coordinated. Initially the invading Chinese Army, and then builders, labourers, miners and administrators were sent to Tibet in order to 'redistribute' Tibet's natural resources.[56]

The ecological effects of this policy have been devastating to the Tibetan environment. Tibet's old-growth forests have been felled and the timber exported to China. Vast portions of Tibet's interior have been transformed into copper and cobalt mines. Huge farming areas—sufficient to support the Tibetan population—have been appropriated and turned into apartments for Han Chinese and shopping centres.[57]

Similarly, China's nuclear weapons and energy programs have degraded Tibet's environment. After it began its nuclear weapons program in 1960, China chose Tibet in which to develop its technology because of its relative geographic seclusion. Unable or unwilling to properly dispose of nuclear waste, China created vast shallow and unlined landfills.[58] These vast contaminated sites, together with a 1984 decision by China to store Europe's nuclear waste in Tibet, have created a potential ecological disaster. (It is a 'potential' disaster because China forbids researchers from entering and studying relevant areas and data.)[59]

China asserts that it does not have a policy of population transfer into Tibet, merely that the 'natural migration' of Han Chinese further into the 'Motherland' is intended to benefit the 'backward' Tibetans.[60]

The reality is, however, very different. Scholars of international law who have managed to gain independent (and secret) access to Tibet report systematic and planned economic discrimination against Tibetans. For example, the construction of the Qinghai–Tibet railroad created 38 000 new jobs. Only 4000, however, were offered to Tibetans, who were promised US$30 a day, but instead received between US$9 and US$12 a day.[61]

---

56   Gyari, L. 1992, *The Tibetan Experience*, Unrepresented Nations and Peoples Organisation Conference on Population Transfer, p. 21.
57   Haertling, 'Trains above the clouds', p. 459.
58   International Campaign for Tibet 1993, *Nuclear Tibet: Nuclear weapons and nuclear waste on the Tibetan Plateau*, International Campaign for Tibet, Washington, DC.
59   Ziemer, L. 2001, 'Application in Tibet of principles on human rights and the environment', *Harvard Human Rights Journal*, vol. 14, p. 261.
60   Information Office of the State Council of the People's Republic of China 1992, *Tibet: Its ownership and human rights situation,* September, Information Office of the State Council of the People's Republic of China, Beijing.
61   Yardley, J. 2003, 'Trying to reshape Tibet: China sends in the masses', *New York Times*, 15 September 2003, p. A1.

In addition, China regularly imposes a policy of excluding Tibetans from certain lucrative primary industry projects. For example, Tibetans are excluded from participating in the construction of hydro-electric dams as well as being prohibited from felling trees—projects that are assigned to Han Chinese.[62]

When these policies are aggregated with Chinese population-planning policies that the 1997 International Commission of Jurists found to include forced abortions and sterilisations, the Tibetans' fear of becoming a minority within their own country seems starkly possible.[63] China's State Department of Planning Commission rejects these concerns, producing 'studies' in rebuttal, with titles such as 'Tibetan population in China: myths and facts re-examined'.[64]

China is well aware of the countless UN resolutions, studies, reports, academic studies, findings of various human rights bodies and the International Commission of Jurists' reports, however, it has repeatedly maintained that international attention on its human rights record, especially towards Tibet, is not appropriate.

China has rejected the universal application of international human rights, instead arguing that it is 'neither appropriate nor workable to demand that all countries measure up to the human rights criteria of one country or a small number of countries'.[65]

Tibet's 'middle-way' proposal

On 10 March 1959, after repeated massacres and destruction by the Chinese military, the Tibetan people rioted. The uprising was quickly and brutally smashed by the army, which then began bombarding the residence of the Dalai Lama.

The fiftieth anniversary of the uprising occurred on 10 March 2008. Riots throughout Tibet were smashed with equal brutality, with reports of summary executions and arbitrary arrest and torture. At a time when China was preparing for the 2008 Summer Olympic Games, it did not want the world's attention drawn to its continuing human rights abuses in occupied Tibet.

In April 2008, His Holiness the XIV Dalai Lama issued an 'appeal to all Chinese spiritual brothers and sisters' to prevent further violence and to assist in the preservation of Tibetan culture in the face of 'cultural genocide'.[66] His Holiness

---

62 Haertling, 'Trains above the clouds', p. 474.
63 International Commission of Jurists, *Tibet*, p. 305 ff.
64 Yan Hao, 'Tibetan population in China', p. 11.
65 Hall, J. 2001, 'Chinese population transfer in Tibet', *Cardozo Journal of International Law*, vol. 9, p. 185.
66 His Holiness the Dalai Lama 2008, An appeal to all Chinese spiritual brothers and sisters, 24 April 2008.

noted the worldwide condemnation of China's brutal response and insisted that the cause of China's concern—that he was seeking independence for Tibet—was unfounded.

China continues to insist that the legality of the relationship between it and Tibet is governed by the Seventeen-Point Agreement that was signed at gunpoint while Chinese troops occupied Lhasa. It was noted above that the agreement was signed by affixing the seal of the Tibetan Government that had been forged by the Chinese 'negotiation' team.

Shortly after escaping the Chinese bombardment of his monastery in Lhasa, His Holiness issued a statement, on 18 April 1959, explaining that the agreement had been signed under duress and that the Chinese Government had deliberately breached the agreement. It was also noted that international-law scholars had vehemently denounced the legality of the agreement and the circumstances in which it was forced on the Tibetan people.[67]

During the 1970s and in place of the Seventeen-Point Agreement, His Holiness began formulating a new approach to the resolution of China's concerns with Tibet.

In September 1987, His Holiness addressed the US Congressional Human Rights Caucus outlining what became known as the 'Five-Point Peace Plan'.[68] This plan was read with His Holiness's 1988 address to members of the European Parliament in Strasbourg, France ('the Strasbourg Proposal').

The Five-Point Peace Plan

The plan contains five basic components that are intended to address most of the concerns discussed above, particularly in removing obstacles to the right of Tibetans to internal and external self-determination. The five components of the plan are

1. transformation of the whole of Tibet into a zone of peace
2. abandonment of China's population-transfer policy, which threatens the very existence of Tibetans as a people
3. respect for the Tibetan people's fundamental human rights and democratic freedoms
4. restoration and protection of Tibet's natural environment and the abandonment of China's use of Tibet for the production of nuclear weapons and dumping of nuclear waste

---

67 Clark, 'China's unlawful control over Tibet', pp. 300–1; Laird, *The Story of* Tibet.
68 His Holiness the Dalai Lama 1987, Five point peace plan, Address to the US Congressional Human Rights Caucus, <http://www.dalailama.com/page.121.htm>

5. commencement of earnest negotiations on the future status of Tibet and relations between the Tibetan and Chinese peoples.

The Strasbourg Proposal

The next year, His Holiness addressed members of the European Parliament in Strasbourg, France. In this address, His Holiness outlined the framework for implementing the Five-Point Peace Plan. The approach of His Holiness contained in these proposals is called the 'middle-way' approach because His Holiness has consistently advocated a middle way between independence and subjugation. His Holiness proposed that Tibet should become a 'self-governing democratic entity' with a democratically elected government responsible for all affairs relating to Tibet and Tibetans. China would maintain control over Tibetan foreign policy.

For his efforts in seeking a peaceful resolution to China's military invasion of Tibet, His Holiness was awarded the Nobel Peace Prize by the international community in 1989.

China's response

Although it initially responded positively to the proposal, the Chinese Government withdrew from all negotiations after the 1989 riots in Tibet and the subsequent massacre of Tibetan protesters. Since 1989, the Chinese Government has continued to demonise His Holiness (referring to the 'Dalai clique') and reject international calls for meaningful negotiations.

China consistently maintains that His Holiness's proposals disguise an ulterior motive of independence—something that is completely unacceptable to China.[69] China therefore accuses the 'Dalai clique' of deception since 'once the Dalai Lama retained power in Tibet, racial discrimination, segregation and purges would be inevitable'.[70]

At the time of the 2008 Beijing Olympics, China manufactured elaborate allegations of plots fomented by His Holiness to 'sabotage the Olympics'. China announced the discovery of 'the secessionists' intention to tarnish the Olympics with the [guidance] of a senior member of the Dalai Clique'.[71]

---

69 Ministry of Foreign Affairs of the People's Republic of China 2003, *What is the Dalai Lama's Middle Way?*, Ministry of Foreign Affairs of the People's Republic of China, Beijing.
70 'China refutes Dalai's so-called "middle way"', *Chinadaily.com*, 10 October 2008.
71 'Dalai coterie's conspiracy aimed at sabotaging Olympics', *People's Daily Online*, 3 July 2008.

While His Holiness has stated publicly his intention to continue negotiations, convinced that only a peaceful solution to the 'Tibet issue' can work, China remains equally convinced that the 'Dalai clique's' proposals are a sham, masking an ulterior motive to regain control of an independent Tibet.

Presently, Hall expresses the situation best:

> China has few incentives to negotiate with Tibet. Barring either the unlikely event of a Soviet-like disintegration of the Chinese empire or a significant increase in global consensus with respect to Tibetan liberation, it is unlikely that Tibet will achieve much leverage anytime soon. Although several nations have called upon China to negotiate with Tibet, China has expressed no interest in doing so.[72]

Conclusion

This chapter began by noting that scholarly research into the position of Tibet in international law seemed to be largely settled in concluding that at the time of the Chinese occupation in 1950, Tibet enjoyed sovereign statehood status. I discovered that as far back as 1954, international private and public scholarship concluded that Tibet was an independent state and that each decade since the 1950 occupation of Tibet had produced further scholarship reaching identical conclusions.

I then examined the legal framework by which Tibetans might assert a right to self-determination in international law. I discussed the basis on which Tibetans were a 'people' within the meaning of that term in international law, entitling them to exercise the right to self-determination.

Concluding that the Tibetans were a people, I then discussed the content of the right to self-determination, drawing the distinction between the 'internal' and 'external' forms of self-determination.

I noted, however, that although the Tibetans possessed the right to self-determination, there was a distinction between external self-determination as self-governance on the one hand and the right to secession on the other. I also discussed the argument that, as a people, Tibetans were under 'colonial or alien subjugation'.

In these circumstances, I concluded that the Tibetans could exercise their external right to self-determination, noting the way international law approached the practical mechanisms for exercising such a right—that of a referendum.

---

72   Hall, 'Chinese population transfer in Tibet', p. 197.

I also highlighted the potential difficulties associated with any attempt by Tibetans to undertake such a referendum. In particular, I discussed the relatively unexplored issue of China's population-transfer policies and the immense cultural and environmental destruction of Tibet.

I then turned to the proposals initiated by His Holiness the Dalai Lama in seeking a peaceful resolution to the Tibet issue through his Five-Point Peace Plan and the Strasbourg Proposal. I explained the content and significance of these proposals and the positive reception they gained in the international community. It is significant that the international community responded by awarding His Holiness the Nobel Peace Prize in 1989.

I then examined China's response to His Holiness's proposals, noting the polemic and rhetoric with which they were dismissed. In particular, the virulent Chinese response to (and rejection of) peace overtures at the time of the 2008 Beijing Olympics was noted.

What to conclude? There is an abundance of international legal scholarship, supplemented by reports of numerous non-governmental organisations, European Parliamentary declarations, UN declarations and private scholarship that attest to Tibet's status in international law.

That scholarship speaks with one voice in concluding that the Chinese invasion of Tibet in 1950 was an egregious violation of international law. Tibet enjoyed de facto if not de jure independence as a state and its citizens were—and remain—a 'people' within the meaning of that term in international law.

Tibet can be regarded as a territory under either 'alien or colonial domination', where that domination by China has resulted in a documented and verified pattern of systematic degradation and human rights abuses.

In these circumstances, while scholars of international law recognise the *theoretical* right of the Tibetan people to self-determination to the point of independence from China, the sad reality is that no state will seek to enforce international law against China. The reasons for this are prudential—motivated largely by economic self-interest in exploiting China's massive and relatively untouched markets.

At the level of international enforcement, China's power in the UN Security Council effectively forecloses any direct action the United Nations might direct against it. Likewise, China has not given authority to the International Court of Justice to hear claims against it. And even if the International Court of Justice were to hear a claim against China, enforcement action by the Security Council under Chapter VII of the UN Charter would be meaningless since China is a permanent member of the council.

In the foreseeable future, therefore, it seems that Tibet will remain oppressed by the People's Republic of China, its rights in international law well recognised but rendered largely meaningless by a combination of economic self-interest and lack of enforcement options by the international community.

Appendix

Summary of the Memorandum on Genuine Autonomy for the Tibetan People

Introduction

During the seventh round of talks in Beijing on 1 and 2 July 2008, the Vice Chairman of the Chinese People's Political Consultative Conference and the Minister of the Central United Front Work Department, Mr Du Qinglin, explicitly invited suggestions from His Holiness the Dalai Lama for the stability and development of Tibet. The Executive Vice Minister of the Central United Front Work Department, Mr Zhu Weiqun, further said they would like to hear our views on the degree or form of autonomy we are seeking as well as on all aspects of regional autonomy within the scope of the *Constitution of the People's Republic of China* (PRC).

Accordingly, during the recent eighth round of talks, we presented the *Memorandum on Genuine Autonomy for the Tibetan People* to the Vice Chairman, Mr Du Qinglin, and held extensive discussions with our Chinese counterparts on November 4th and 5th in Beijing.

In recent days the Central United Front Work Department of the Chinese Communist Party has issued statements about our talks in Beijing and in particular about the content of the memorandum we have presented to them. These Chinese statements distort the position and proposal we have outlined in our paper. In order to enable the public, concerned governments, parliamentarians, non-governmental organisations and individuals to gain a comprehensive and full understanding of the Tibetan position on genuine autonomy for the Tibetan people, we are releasing today the memorandum.

Our memorandum puts forth our position on genuine autonomy and how the specific needs of the Tibetan nationality for autonomy and self-government can be met through application of the principles on autonomy of the *Constitution of the People's Republic of China*, as we understand them. On this basis, His Holiness the Dalai Lama felt confident that the basic needs of the Tibetan nationality can be met through genuine autonomy within the PRC.

Summary of the memorandum

The *Constitution of the PRC* contains fundamental principles on autonomy and self-government whose objectives are compatible with the needs and aspirations of the Tibetans. Regional national autonomy is aimed at opposing both the oppression and the separation of nationalities by rejecting both Han chauvinism and local nationalism. It is intended to ensure the protection of the culture and the identity of minority nationalities by empowering them to become masters of their own affairs.

To a very considerable extent Tibetan needs can be met within the constitutional principles on autonomy. On several points, the Constitution gives significant discretionary powers to state organs in decision-making and on the operation of the system of autonomy. These discretionary powers can be exercised to facilitate genuine autonomy for Tibetans in ways that would respond to the uniqueness of the Tibetan situation.

Given good will on both sides, outstanding problems can be resolved within the constitutional principles on autonomy. In this way national unity and stability and harmonious relations between the Tibetan and other nationalities will be established.

Tibetan aspirations

Tibetans have a rich and distinct history, culture and spiritual tradition all of which form valuable parts of the heritage of humanity. Not only do Tibetans wish to preserve their own heritage, which they cherish, but equally they wish to further develop their culture and spiritual life and knowledge in ways that are particularly suited to the needs and conditions of humanity in the 21st century.

As a part of the multi-national state of the PRC, Tibetans can benefit greatly from the rapid economic and scientific development the country is experiencing. While wanting to actively participate and contribute to this development, we want to ensure that this happens without the people losing their Tibetan identity, culture and core values and without putting the distinct and fragile environment of the Tibetan Plateau, to which Tibetans are indigenous, at risk.

His Holiness the Dalai Lama's commitment to seek a solution for the Tibetan people within the PRC is clear and unambiguous. This position is in full compliance and agreement with paramount leader Deng Xiaoping's statement in which he emphasised that except for independence all other issues could be resolved through dialogue. Whereas, we are committed, therefore, to fully respect the territorial integrity of the PRC, we expect the Central Government to recognise and fully respect the integrity of the Tibetan nationality and its right to exercise genuine autonomy within the PRC. We believe that this is the basis for resolving the differences between us and promoting unity, stability and harmony among nationalities.

Appendix

Basic needs of Tibetans

Subject matters of self-government

1. Language
2. Culture
3. Religion
4. Education
5. Environmental protection
6. Utilisation of natural resources
7. Economic development and trade
8. Public health
9. Public security
10. Regulation on population migration
11. Cultural, educational and religious exchanges with other countries

Respect for the integrity of the Tibetan nationality

Tibetans belong to one minority nationality regardless of the current administrative divisions. The integrity of the Tibetan nationality must be respected. That is the spirit, the intent and the principle underlying the constitutional concept of national regional autonomy as well as the principle of equality of nationalities.

There is no dispute about the fact that Tibetans share the same language, culture, spiritual tradition, core values and customs, that they belong to the same ethnic group and that they have a strong sense of common identity. Tibetans share a common history and despite periods of political or administrative divisions, Tibetans continuously remained united by their religion, culture, education, language, way of life and by their unique high plateau environment.

The Tibetan nationality lives in one contiguous area on the Tibetan Plateau, which they have inhabited for millennia and to which they are therefore indigenous. For purposes of the constitutional principles of national regional autonomy Tibetans in the PRC in fact live as a single nationality all over the Tibetan Plateau.

In order for the Tibetan nationality to develop and flourish with its distinct identity, culture and spiritual tradition through the exercise of self-government on the above mentioned basic Tibetan needs, the entire community, comprising all the areas currently designated by the PRC as Tibetan autonomous areas, should be under one single administrative entity. The current administrative divisions, by which Tibetan communities are ruled and administered under different provinces and regions of the PRC, foments fragmentation, promotes unequal development, and weakens the ability of the Tibetan nationality to protect and promote its common cultural, spiritual and ethnic identity. Rather than respecting the integrity of the nationality, this policy promotes its fragmentation and disregards the spirit of autonomy.

The nature and structure of the autonomy

The exercise of genuine autonomy would include the right of Tibetans to create their own regional government and government institutions and processes that are best suited to their needs and characteristics.

It would require that the People's Congress of the autonomous region have the power to legislate on all matters within the competencies of the region and that other organs of the autonomous government have the power to execute and administer decisions autonomously. Autonomy also entails representation and meaningful participation in national decision-making in the Central Government. Processes for effective consultation and close cooperation or joint decision-making between the Central Government and the regional government on areas of common interest also need to be in place for the autonomy to be effective.

A crucial element of genuine autonomy is the guarantee the Constitution or other laws provide that powers and responsibilities allocated to the autonomous region cannot be unilaterally abrogated or changed. This means that neither the Central Government nor the autonomous region's government should be able, without the consent of the other, to change the basic features of the autonomy.

Implementation of genuine autonomy, for example, requires clear divisions of powers and responsibilities between the Central Government and the government of the autonomous region with respect to subject matter competency. Currently there is no such clarity and the scope of legislative powers of autonomous regions is both uncertain and severely restricted. Thus, whereas the Constitution intends to recognise the special need for autonomous regions to legislate on many matters that affect them, the requirements of Article 116 for prior approval at the highest level of the Central Government—by the Standing Committee of National People's Congress (NPC)—inhibit the implementation of this principle of autonomy. In reality, it is only autonomous regional congresses that expressly require such approval, while the congresses of ordinary (not autonomous) provinces of the PRC do not need prior permission and merely report the passage of regulations to the Standing Committee of the NPC 'for the record' (Article 100).

Appendix

The exercise of autonomy is further subject to a considerable number of laws and regulations, according to Article 115 of the Constitution. Certain laws effectively restrict the autonomy of the autonomous region, while others are not always consistent with one another. The result is that the exact scope of the autonomy is unclear and is not fixed, since it is unilaterally changed with the enactment of laws and regulations at higher levels of the state, and even by changes in policy. There is also no adequate process for consultation or for settling differences that arise between the organs of the Central Government and of the regional government with respect to the scope and exercise of autonomy. In practice, the resulting uncertainty limits the initiative of regional authorities and impedes the exercise of genuine autonomy by Tibetans today.

— Dharamsala, 16 November 2008

His Holiness the Dalai Lama responds to the vote of thanks.

His Holiness gestures to Venerable Alex Bruce.

Participants' details

His Holiness the Dalai Lama

His Holiness, the fourteenth Dalai Lama, Tenzin Gyatso, is a head of state and a spiritual leader. He was born to a peasant family on 6 July 1935 in the small village of Takster in the north-eastern province of Amdo. At the age of two, he was recognised as the reincarnation of the thirteenth Dalai Lama and, at the age of six, began his monastic education in Lhasa, qualifying in 1959 as a '*Geshe*' or Doctor of Buddhist Philosophy.

After the 1950 Chinese invasion of Tibet, the Dalai Lama was called on to take full political responsibility as Head of State and Government of Tibet. The Chinese military presence continued to build and, in March 1959, rumours spread throughout Lhasa that the Chinese Military would kidnap the Dalai Lama. By the morning of 10 March, huge crowds of Tibetans had gathered outside the Norbulingka, the Dalai Lama's summer palace, with the intention of protecting him. This was the beginning of the Tibetan uprising against the Chinese in Tibet. During the two weeks of the uprising, more than 87 000 Tibetans died.

During the uprising, the Dalai Lama and his immediate family escaped from Lhasa in disguise across the border into India, where he was granted asylum. Approximately 80 000 Tibetans followed him into exile. The Indian Government offered the Dalai Lama a home in Dharamsala, a small town in the foothills of the Himalayas in the northern Indian state of Himachal Pradesh.

The Dalai Lama has frequently maintained that his personal preference would be to retire from his political role and concentrate instead on his spiritual role. The plight of his people inside Tibet has, however, made this impossible. He continues to travel the world giving Buddhist teachings and talks on a wide variety of spiritual and ethical topics and urging world leaders to assist him in bringing about a resolution to the Tibetan situation.

In 1989, the Dalai Lama was awarded the Nobel Peace Prize for his peaceful struggle for the liberation of Tibet. The award cites his unwavering commitment to non-violence and his tireless search for 'peaceful solutions based upon tolerance and mutual respect in order to preserve the historical and cultural heritage of his people'. Although the Dalai Lama describes himself as a simple Buddhist monk, people who meet him immediately recognise an individual of profound scholarship and integrity who exerts an extraordinarily enlightened presence with his warmth and universal wisdom. His message is one of love, compassion and tolerance:

Every human being is a member of humanity and the human family, regardless of differences in religion, culture, colour and creed. I am serving our cause with the motivation of service to humankind, not for reasons of power, not out of hatred. Not just as a Tibetan, but as a human being my mission is the propagation of true kindness, genuine kindness and compassion.

Rabbi Jonathan Keren-Black, Leo Baeck Centre, Melbourne

Rabbi Jonathan Keren-Black was born in London and grew up in a committed progressive Jewish family. After studying and working as an engineer, Rabbi Keren-Black completed five years of rabbinical training in Israel and Australia. After his ordination in 1988, Rabbi Keren-Black spent 15 years in a congregation in London and was also involved in establishing pluralist Jewish schools.

In 2003, Rabbi Keren-Black moved to his position at the Leo Baeck Centre in Melbourne. Presently, he has a congregation of nearly 300 households forming part of the Union for Progressive Judaism. He is heavily involved in environmental work and in the Jewish Christian Muslim Association of Australia, which runs residential conferences, school programs and other events.

Judaism

Too many people believe religion is the cause of the world's problems. This belief poses difficult questions for today's religious leaders; why can't we get our religious messages across? A fundamental message Judaism teaches us is 'seek peace and pursue it'. We must all work for peace. How to create peace? Judaism teaches that God created everyone in fundamental equality, that everyone—whether man or woman, brown or white skinned, rich or poor—carries the image of God. Judaism maintains that there are multiple ways to God. These ways are characterised by the use of our gift of wisdom to extend our care and compassion, our love and acceptance, to every person. In this way, we all travel our various paths to God and to true peace.

Most Reverend Bishop Christopher Prowse, Catholic Archdiocese of Melbourne

Bishop Christopher Prowse is the Auxiliary Bishop of the Archdiocese of Melbourne. He was born and educated in Melbourne, and completed a Doctorate in Moral Theology from the Lateran University (Alphonsianum) in 1995.

Bishop Prowse has been involved in numerous inter-religious dialogues in recent years, representing the Catholic Church in Melbourne in Islamic, Jewish and Buddhist discussions.

Friendship

Friendship is an expression that can be described simplistically in sentimental or individualistic terms. Friendship, properly understood, however, can serve as the basis for the respect and commitment that religions of the world have for each other. Here friendship responds to mutual desire and works creatively over a long period to break down barriers and celebrate love.

Friendship defends human dignity and rights. It condemns outright caricatures of itself as a pretext for war or terrorist acts. It embraces the common good. Friendship is motivated by compassion and works towards a global peace ethic. It is ready to see 'the other' not as a threat but as a brother or sister who 'completes' me. It desires that the poor and marginalised come into the centre of the circle of life. It is ready to forgive and show mercy. It acknowledges the beauty of all creation and strives to respect it.

Christians believe that through an encounter with Jesus Christ, as Redeemer and Saviour, the foundation of the full truth of friendship is unlocked. Together with all religions and all men and women of goodwill, Christians desire to build continuously a culture of peace that dispels the midnight of war and welcomes the dawn of peace.

Professor Abdullah Saeed, Sultan of Oman Professor of Arab and Islamic Studies and Director of the Asia Institute, University of Melbourne; and Director of the National Centre of Excellence for Islamic Studies

Professor Saeed's main area of research is Islamic thought, on which he has published numerous works including *Islamic Thought: An introduction*, *Interpreting the Qur'an: Towards a contemporary approach*, *Freedom of Religion, Apostasy and Islam* and *Islam in Australia*.

Professor Saeed's experience in engaging with the Muslim, Christian and Jewish communities, to enhance community understandings of Islam, Islamic thought and Muslim societies, places him well to contribute to this dialogue.

Islam and the message of peace and compassion

Professor Saeed explores the message of peace and compassion that is at the heart of Islamic foundation texts and tradition, utilising examples from the Qur'an, the practice of the Prophet Muhammad and Muslims as well as generally accepted norms and values of Islam.

Despite the vast array of ideas, principles and practices in Islam that are directly connected to peace and compassion, there are some who go against these very foundations of the faith and have adopted a discourse and practice that rely on hatred, enmity and lack of compassion, adopting violence and creating havoc, and justifying their behaviour in the name of Islam. This message of hatred and violence is counter to the overall ethos of Islam. There needs to be an emphasis on the overwhelming message of peace and compassion inherent in Islam, which brings together people of all backgrounds, faiths and cultures under the banner of a shared humanity.

Venerable Alex Bruce, Senior Lecturer, ANU College of Law, and Buddhist monk

Venerable Alex Bruce is a Senior Lecturer at the ANU College of Law and a Buddhist monk ordained into the Tibetan tradition of His Holiness the Dalai Lama. Between 1999 and 2004, Venerable Alex alternated working with the Australian Competition and Consumer Commission as a senior lawyer and teaching at The Australian National University.

This symposium originated from Alex's concern for the role of inter-religious dialogue in creating a peaceful and enlightened future. Alex has Masters degrees in law from the University of Sydney and in theology from the Australian Catholic University.

Alex hopes one day to establish an institution where Islamic, Jewish, Christian and Buddhist scholars can engage in dialogue, translation, prayer and teaching in order to dispel ignorance and fear of one another's traditions.

ANU College of Law

The One World—Many Paths to Peace Inter-faith Dialogue was presented by the ANU College of Law, part of The Australian National University. The Australian National University, ranked as Australia's premier university and as one of the best in the world, was created by an act of Federal Parliament in 1946 to drive social, cultural and economic prosperity, and to advance Australia's international standing through high-quality research and education.

The Australian National University is distinctive because of its national mission, international focus and long record of success in research and education for undergraduate and postgraduate students. As the national university in the national capital, The Australian National University is engaged distinctively with the civic and commercial life of Canberra and Australia.

The ANU College of Law is one of Australia's leading law schools. The college has produced graduates who are now leaders in their chosen fields all over the world. It is also home to some of Australia's best-known and most outstanding legal scholars and teachers and to flagship publications such as the *Federal Law Review* and the *Australian Year Book of International Law*.

The college also includes the Legal Workshop and a number of associated centres and affiliated bodies.

Located in the national capital, the seat of the national parliament and the High Court of Australia, the ANU College of Law is, in a sense, Australia's 'national' law school. Accordingly, it has special strengths in a number of areas, including international law and public law. The college draws its students and staff from all over Australia, as well as from overseas. It has not only the traditional commitment of Australian law schools to excellence in teaching and research, but a distinct ethos of commitment to social justice and the continuous improvement of the law.

The ANU College of Law offers a range of undergraduate and postgraduate programs, including the LLB, Graduate Diploma and Masters programs, practical legal training through the Legal Workshop and research degrees such as the SJD and PhD. These programs incorporate a number of special opportunities such as internships, clinical programs, overseas exchanges, supervised research and writing, intensive courses and access to cutting-edge research and scholarship.

To find out more about the ANU College of Law, go to <http://law.anu.edu.au>

One World—Many Paths to Peace

Left–right: Professor Abdullah Saeed (at lectern), Venerable Alex Bruce, Rabbi Jonathan Keren-Black, translator to His Holiness, His Holiness the Dalai Lama, Bishop Christopher Prowse.

The audience at the AIS Arena.

Participants' details

His Holiness the Dalai Lama thanks Rabbi Jonathan Keren-Black.

His Holiness the Dalai Lama thanks Bishop Christopher Prowse.

One World—Many Paths to Peace

His Holiness the Dalai Lama thanks Professor Abdullah Saeed.

Venerable Buddhist Sangha.

Participants' details

Professor Michael Coper, Dean, ANU College of Law.

One World—Many Paths to Peace

Venerable Alex Bruce, creator and moderator of the symposium.

Participants' details

His Holiness the Dalai Lama emphasises tolerance, peace and wisdom.

www.ingramcontent.com/pod-product-compliance
Lightning Source LLC
Chambersburg PA
CBHW060947170426
43197CB00031B/2984